EVERYTHING YOU NEED TO KNOW ABOUT MATH HOMEWORK

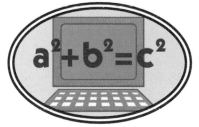

$$a^2+b^2=c^2$$

Anne Zeman and Kate Kelly

An Irving Place Press Book

Scholastic
Reference

New York   Toronto   London   Auckland   Sydney

Design: Bennett Gewirtz, Gewirtz Graphics, Inc.
Illustration: Moffitt Cecil

For their assistance in the preparation of this manuscript, grateful acknowledgment to Betty Holmes, Director of UFT's Dial-A-Teacher, and Tom Scarpinato, Rich Gross, and Jeanne Willis. Dial-A-Teacher is a collaborative program of the United Federation of Teachers and the New York City Board of Education.

Library of Congress Cataloging-in-Publication Data

Zeman, Anne, 1951-
   Everything you need to know about math homework / Anne Zeman
and Kate Kelly.
      p.   cm. — (Scholastic homework reference series)
   Includes index.
   ISBN 0-590-49358-2
   1. Mathematics—Study and teaching—Juvenile literature.
   2. Homework—Juvenile literature. [1. Mathematics. 2. Homework.]
   I. Kelly, Kate. II. Title. III. Series.
   QA11.Z46   1994
   510—dc20   93-49351
                                                                       CIP
                                                                        AC

12 11 10 9 8 7 6 5 4 3 2 1   4 5 6 7 8 9/9

Printed in the U.S.A.   09
First Scholastic printing, August 1994

CONTENTS

INTRODUCTION

It's homework time—but you have questions. Just how did your teacher ask you to do the assignment? You need help, but your parents are busy, and you can't reach your classmate on the phone. Where can you go for help?

What Questions Does This Book Answer?

In *Everything You Need to Know About Math Homework*, you will find a wealth of information, including the answers to ten of the most commonly asked math homework questions.*

1. What are prime numbers? You'll find a definition and a list of prime numbers up to 100 on page 7.

2. How do you change a base 10 numeral into base 2 or base 5? A table and a step-by-step explanation of converting base 10 to base 2 and 5 is found on pages 19-20.

3. How do you do long division? You'll find the procedure explained—with several examples—on page 36.

4. How do you find the lowest common denominator of two or more fractions? Look up the answer on page 41.

5. How do you reduce fractions to lowest terms? The procedure is explained on page 41.

6. How do you calculate percentages, find a number when only its percentage is known, or figure out what percent one number is of another? All these calculations are explained with examples on pages 48-49.

7. How do you round off to the nearest 10, 100, or 1,000? Rounding off is explained on pages 50-51.

8. How do you change centimeters to meters or feet to inches? Look at the measurement tables of pages 64-65.

9. How do you measure angles? See page 96.

10. How do you make a bar graph or a line graph? How do you read graphs that are already made? A complete explanation of creating and reading graphs is found on pages 112-117.

* According to Dial-A-Teacher

What Is the Scholastic Homework Reference Series?

The Scholastic Homework Reference Series is a set of unique reference resources written especially to answer the homework questions of fourth, fifth, and sixth graders. The series provides ready information to answer commonly asked homework questions in a variety of subjects. Here you'll find facts, charts, definitions, and explanations, complete with examples and illustrations that will supplement schoolwork colorfully, clearly—and comprehensively.

A Note to Parents

The information for the Scholastic Homework Reference Series was gathered from current textbooks, national curricula, and the invaluable assistance of the UFT Dial-A-Teacher staff. Dial-A-Teacher, a collaborative program of the United Federation of Teachers and the New York City Board of Education, is a telephone service available to elementary school students in New York City. Telephone lines are open during the school term from 4:00 to 7:00 p.m., Monday to Thursday, by dialing 212-777-3380. Because of Dial-A-Teacher's success in New York City, similar organizations have been established in other communities across the country. Check to see if there's a telephone homework service in your area.

It's important to support your children's efforts to do homework. Welcome their questions and see that they are equipped with a well-lighted desk or table, pencils, paper, and any other books or equipment—such as rulers, calculators, reference or text books, and so on—that they may need. You might also set aside a special time each day for doing homework, a time when you're available to answer questions that may arise. But don't do your children's homework for them. Remember, homework should create a bond between school and home. It is meant to enhance on a daily basis the lessons taught at school, and to promote good work and study habits. Although it is gratifying to have your children present flawless homework papers, the flawlessness should be a result of your children's explorations and efforts—not your own.

The Scholastic Homework Reference Series is designed to help your children complete their homework on their own to the best of their abilities. If they're stuck, you can use these books with them to find answers to troubling homework problems. And, remember, when the work is done—praise your children for a job well done.

EVERYTHING YOU NEED TO KNOW ABOUT MATH HOMEWORK

NUMBERS AND NUMBER SYSTEMS

1 Ancient Number Systems

Who Invented Numbers?

Who invented numbers? No one knows for sure, but the use of numbers may have started as far back as cave people. In order to keep track of tools or skins, a caveperson might have matched each tool or skin with a finger. If there were more tools or skins than fingers, the caveperson might have picked up pebbles. Each pebble would be used to stand for one tool or skin.

Tally Systems

Matching pebbles to things is one kind of *tally system*. Early tally systems were used to keep track of the days between full moons. This was how our ancestors kept time. The tally system was improved by grouping tally markers in fives–pebbles, lines, etc.

The word *calculate* comes from the Latin word *calculus*, which means "pebble."

Digits to Base 10

Another counting word is *digit*. A digit is any of the numerals from *1* to *9*. The word "digit" is also the name for a finger. So number digits can be counted on finger digits.

The ancient Romans used a counting system that combined *base 5* and *base 10* (see p. 19). Our modern system of counting is a base 10 system. Both base 5 and base 10 probably come from counting on fingers. Fingers and hands were among the earliest known calculators!

Most people in the world use a base 10 counting system, and most languages of the world use words for "hand" and "finger" as counting words. The Russian word for "five" is *pyat*. *Pyad* means "hand with fingers spread out." In Persian, "five" is *pantcha* and "hand" is *pentcha*. In Old English, *endleofan*, or eleven, means "ten digits [fingers] with one left over," and *twelf*, or twelve, means "ten digits [fingers] with two left over."

Using Fingers and Toes?

The Mayans, an ancient Central American culture, developed a base 20 counting system. In addition to counting on their fingers, they probably used their toes.

Zero

The Mayans also created a numeral for zero. So did Hindu astronomers in India. It took the rest of the world about 800 years to catch on to the idea of *zero*, or "nothing."

ARABIC

1
2
3
4
5
6
7
8
9
10

NUMBER SYSTEMS

EGYPTIAN	IONIC & IONIC GREEK	BABYLONIAN	HEBREW	CHINESE	MAYAN	ROMAN

A CLOSER LOOK AT ROMAN NUMERALS

Roman numerals were created over 2,000 years ago. They are still used today. You can find Roman numerals on clock and watch faces, on monuments and building inscriptions, and on official papers, magazines, and books.

The Roman numeral system uses seven letters to represent numbers. Combinations of these letters represent other numbers.

I	=	1
V	=	5
X	=	10
L	=	50
C	=	100
D	=	500
M	=	1,000

A bar over a Roman numeral tells you to multiply the value by 1,000.

$\overline{I}$	=	1,000
$\overline{V}$	=	5,000
$\overline{X}$	=	10,000
$\overline{L}$	=	50,000
$\overline{C}$	=	100,000
$\overline{D}$	=	500,000
$\overline{M}$	=	1,000,000

Combining Roman Numerals

To make the Roman numeral for 2, I is added to I, so II = 2 (and II + I = III, or 3).

1 = I

2 = I + I or II

3 = I + I + I or III

When a letter representing a number of lesser value appears to the left of a letter of greater value, the lesser value is subtracted from the greater value.

To make the Roman 4, subtract one from five, or V – I = IV.

4 = V – I or IV

five minus one　　one less than five

9 = X – I or IX

ten minus one　　one less than ten

49 = L – I or IL

fifty minus one　　one less than fifty

90 = C – X or XC

one hundred minus ten　　ten less than one hundred

1 = I	8 = VIII	104 = CIV
2 = II	9 = IX	105 = CV
3 = III	10 = X	106 = CVI
4 = IV	11 = XI	107 = CVII
5 = V	12 = XII	108 = CVIII
6 = VI	13 = XIII	109 = CIX
7 = VII	14 = XIV	110 = CX
	15 = XV	120 = CXX
	16 = XVI	130 = CXXX
	17 = XVII	140 = CXL
	18 = XVIII	150 = CL
	19 = XIX	160 = CLX
	20 = XX	170 = CLXX
	30 = XXX	180 = CLXXX
	40 = XL	190 = CXC
	50 = L	200 = CC
	60 = LX	300 = CCC
	70 = LXX	400 = CD
	80 = LXXX	500 = D
	90 = XC	600 = DC
	100 = C	700 = DCC
	101 = CI	800 = DCCC
	102 = CII	900 = CM
	103 = CIII	1,000 = M

2 The Decimal System

The *decimal system* uses ten symbols: *0, 1, 2, 3, 4, 5, 6, 7, 8,* and *9*. The word "decimal" comes from the Latin root *decem*, meaning "ten." Within the decimal system are many different kinds of number groupings, called *number sets*. The number sets include: *counting numbers*, *rational numbers*, *prime numbers*, *composite numbers*, *even* and *odd numbers*, and *integers*.

Arabic into Decimal

The numerals we use today are called *decimal* numerals. These numerals stand for the numbers in the decimal system. The decimal system is also known as the Arabic system. The decimal system was first created by Hindu astronomers in India over a thousand years ago. It spread into Europe around 700 years ago. Here's how the Hindu numerals have changed to become our modern numeral system:

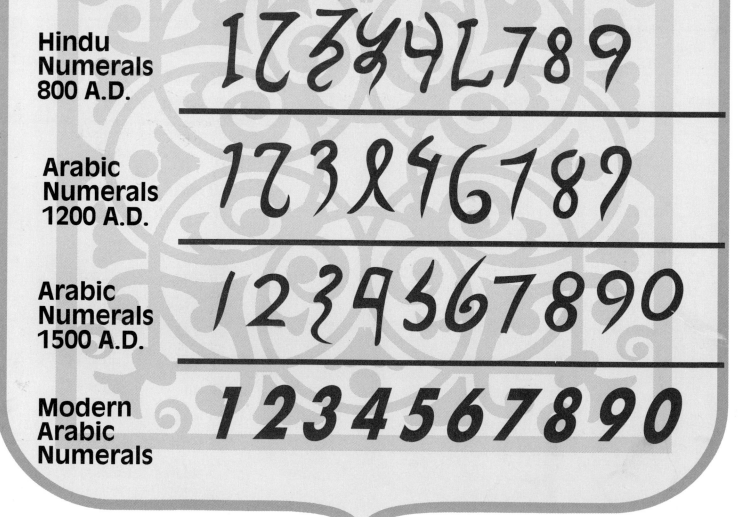

Hindu Numerals 800 A.D.

Arabic Numerals 1200 A.D.

Arabic Numerals 1500 A.D.

Modern Arabic Numerals

Number Sets

Counting Numbers

The set of *counting numbers*, or *natural numbers*, begins with the number *1* and continues into infinity.

{1, 2, 3, 4, 5, 6, 7, 8, 9, 10 . . .}

Whole Numbers

The set of *whole numbers* is the same as the set of counting numbers, except that it begins with *0*.

{0, 1, 2, 3, 4, 5, 6, 7, 8, 9, 10 . . .}

 All counting numbers are whole numbers. Zero is the only whole number that is not a counting number.

Rational Numbers

The set of *rational numbers* includes any number that can be written in the form of a *fraction* (see Fractions, p. 39), as long as the *denominator* (or bottom number of the fraction) is not equal to *0*.

 All counting numbers and whole numbers can be written as fractions with a denominator equal to 1. That means that all counting numbers and whole numbers are also rational numbers.

Prime Numbers

Prime numbers are counting numbers that can be divided by only two numbers—*1* and themselves. A prime number can also be described as a counting number with only two *factors*, *1* and itself (see p. 22). The number *1*, because it can be divided only by itself, is *not* a prime number.

Prime Numbers to 100
2, 3, 5, 7, 11, 13, 17, 19, 23, 29, 31, 37, 41, 43, 47,
53, 59, 61, 67, 71, 73, 79, 83, 89, 97

The set of counting numbers has no end. It can go on forever. The idea that counting numbers can go on and on is called *infinity*. Infinity has a special symbol:

There is no such thing as the "largest number." You can always add to or multiply a large number to make an even bigger number.

∞ + 3 = ∞

∞ x 10 = ∞

If you began writing all the counting numbers today, you could continue writing every moment of every day for every day of the rest of your life and never be finished!

Fibonacci Numbers

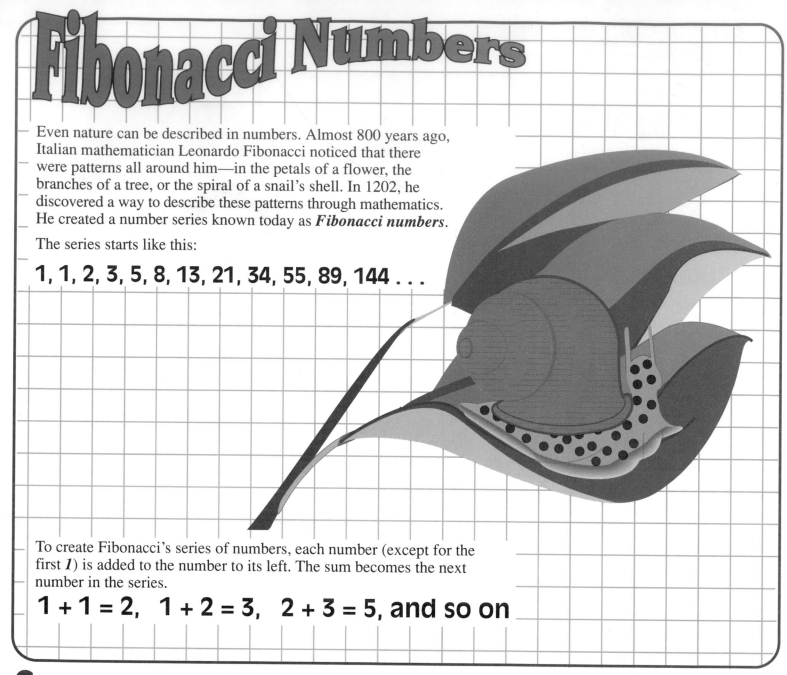

Even nature can be described in numbers. Almost 800 years ago, Italian mathematician Leonardo Fibonacci noticed that there were patterns all around him—in the petals of a flower, the branches of a tree, or the spiral of a snail's shell. In 1202, he discovered a way to describe these patterns through mathematics. He created a number series known today as *Fibonacci numbers*.

The series starts like this:

1, 1, 2, 3, 5, 8, 13, 21, 34, 55, 89, 144 . . .

To create Fibonacci's series of numbers, each number (except for the first *1*) is added to the number to its left. The sum becomes the next number in the series.

1 + 1 = 2,   1 + 2 = 3,   2 + 3 = 5, and so on

Composite Numbers

Composite numbers are all counting numbers that are not prime numbers. In other words, composite numbers are numbers that have more than two *factors* (see p. 22). The number *1*, because it has only one factor (itself), is *not* a composite number.

Composite Numbers to 100

4, 6, 8, 9, 10, 12, 14, 15, 16, 18, 20, 21, 22, 24, 25, 26, 27, 28, 30, 32, 33, 34, 35, 36, 38, 39, 40, 42, 44, 45, 46, 48, 49, 50, 51, 52, 54, 55, 56, 57, 58, 60, 62, 63, 64, 65, 66, 68, 69, 70, 72, 74, 75, 76, 77, 78, 80, 81, 82, 84, 85, 86, 87, 88, 90, 91, 92, 93, 94, 95, 96, 98, 99, 100

Even and Odd Numbers

Even numbers include the numbers *0* and *2* and all numbers that can be divided evenly by *2*. *Odd numbers* are all numbers that cannot be divided evenly by *2*.

Odd and Even Numbers to 100

0 1 2 3 4 5 6 7 8 9 10 11 12 13 14 15 16 17 18 19 20 21 22 23

24 25 26 27 28 29 30 31 32 33 34 35 36 37 38 39 40 41 42 43

44 45 46 47 48 49 50 51 52 53 54 55 56 57 58 59 60 61 62 63

64 65 66 67 68 69 70 71 72 73 74 75 76 77 78 79 80 81 82 83

84 85 86 87 88 89 90 91 92 93 94 95 96 97 98 99 100

Integers

The set of *integers* includes *0*, all of the counting numbers (called *positive* whole numbers), and the whole numbers less than *0* (called *negative* whole numbers). Integers are shown below on a number line.

 All counting numbers and whole numbers are integers.

Numbers less than **0** are negative numbers.   Numbers greater than **0** are positive numbers.

Absolute Value

Absolute value tells the distance of a positive or negative number from *0*.
Absolute value is always stated as a positive number.

> The symbol *| |* means absolute value. For example, *|−3| = 3 (or the
> absolute value of minus 3 is 3). |3| is 3 (or the absolute value of 3 is 3).*

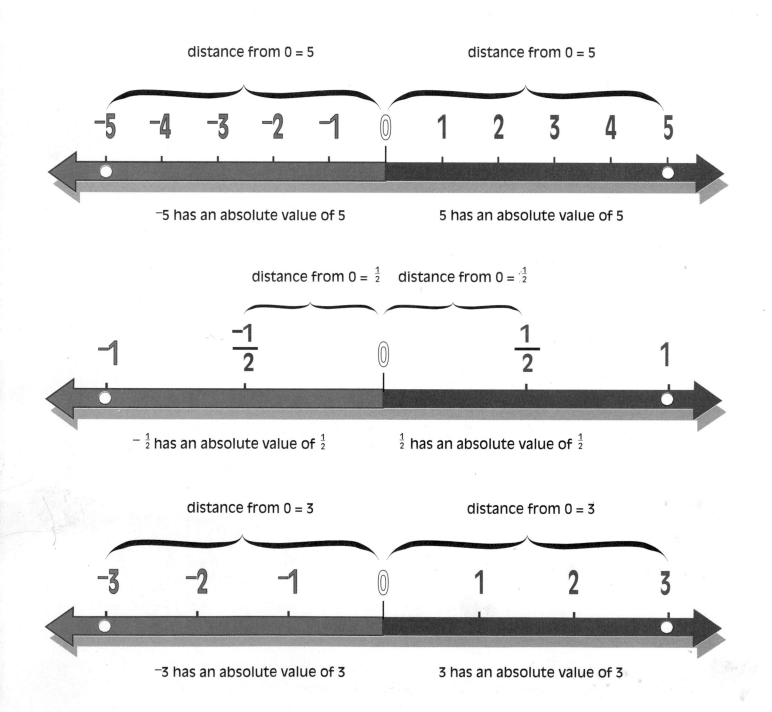

distance from 0 = 5   distance from 0 = 5

−5   −4   −3   −2   −1   0   1   2   3   4   5

−5 has an absolute value of 5   5 has an absolute value of 5

distance from 0 = $\frac{1}{2}$ distance from 0 = $\frac{1}{2}$

−1 $\frac{-1}{2}$ 0 $\frac{1}{2}$ 1

$-\frac{1}{2}$ has an absolute value of $\frac{1}{2}$ $\frac{1}{2}$ has an absolute value of $\frac{1}{2}$

distance from 0 = 3   distance from 0 = 3

−3   −2   −1   0   1   2   3

−3 has an absolute value of 3   3 has an absolute value of 3

What's a GOOGOL?

A googol is the number **1** followed by 100 zeroes.

10,000,000,000,000,000,000,
000,000,000,000,000,000,000,
000,000,000,000,000,000,000,
000,000,000,000,000,000,000,
000,000,000,000,000,000

American mathematician Edward Kasner needed to solve a problem using enormous numbers. His nine-year-old nephew made up the term "googol." Dr. Kasner made up the word "googolplex" to mean **1** followed by a googol of zeros! Googol and googolplex are more simply written in *exponents* (see p. 24). The googolplex is the largest named number.

BIGGER THAN A

1,000,000,000 Billion
1,000,000,000,000 Trillion
1,000,000,000,000,000 Quadrillion
1,000,000,000,000,000,000 Quintillion
1,000,000,000,000,000,000,000 Sextillion
1,000,000,000,000,000,000,000,000 Septillion
1,000,000,000,000,000,000,000,000,000 Octillion
1,000,000,000,000,000,000,000,000,000,000 Nonillion
1,000,000,000,000,000,000,000,000,000,000,000 Decillion
1,000,000,000,000,000,000,000,000,000,000,000,000 Undecillion
1,000,000,000,000,000,000,000,000,000,000,000,000,000 Duodecillion
1,000,000,000,000,000,000,000,000,000,000,000,000,000,000 Tredecillion
1,000,000,000,000,000,000,000,000,000,000,000,000,000,000,000 Quarthordecillion
1,000,000,000,000,000,000,000,000,000,000,000,000,000,000,000,000 Qumdecillion
1,000,000,000,000,000,000,000,000,000,000,000,000,000,000,000,000,000 Sexdecillion
1,000,000,000,000,000,000,000,000,000,000,000,000,000,000,000,000,000,000 Septdecillion
1,000,000,000,000,000,000,000,000,000,000,000,000,000,000,000,000,000,000,000 Octodecillion
1,000,000,000,000,000,000,000,000,000,000,000,000,000,000,000,000,000,000,000,000 Novemdecillion
1,000,000,000,000,000,000,000,000,000,000,000,000,000,000,000,000,000,000,000,000,000 Vigintillion

10,000,000,000,000,000,000,
000,000,000,000,000,000,000,000,
000,000,000,000,000,000,000,000,000,
000,000,000,000,000,000,000,000,000,000

GOOGOL

Sets

A *set* is a collection of items, for instance: coins, marbles, dishes, trading cards, or even numbers! Items within a set are called **members of the set**. There are three types of sets: equal sets, equivalent sets, and subsets.

Equal sets are sets that have identical members.

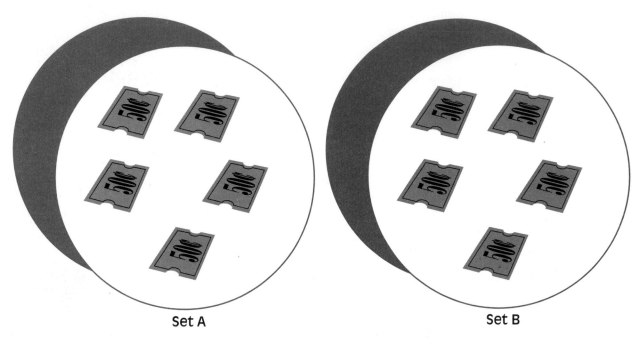

Set A   Set B

Sets A and B are equal sets

Members Only, Please!

Braces { and } are used to show members of a set.

Members of the set of refreshment stand goodies = {popcorn, soda, hot dogs, cotton candy}

Equivalent sets are sets that have the same number of members.

Set C

Set D

Sets C and D are equivalent sets

Subsets are sets contained within other sets.

Set E

Set F

Set E is a subset of Set C
Set F is a subset of Set D

∪ means "union of sets"

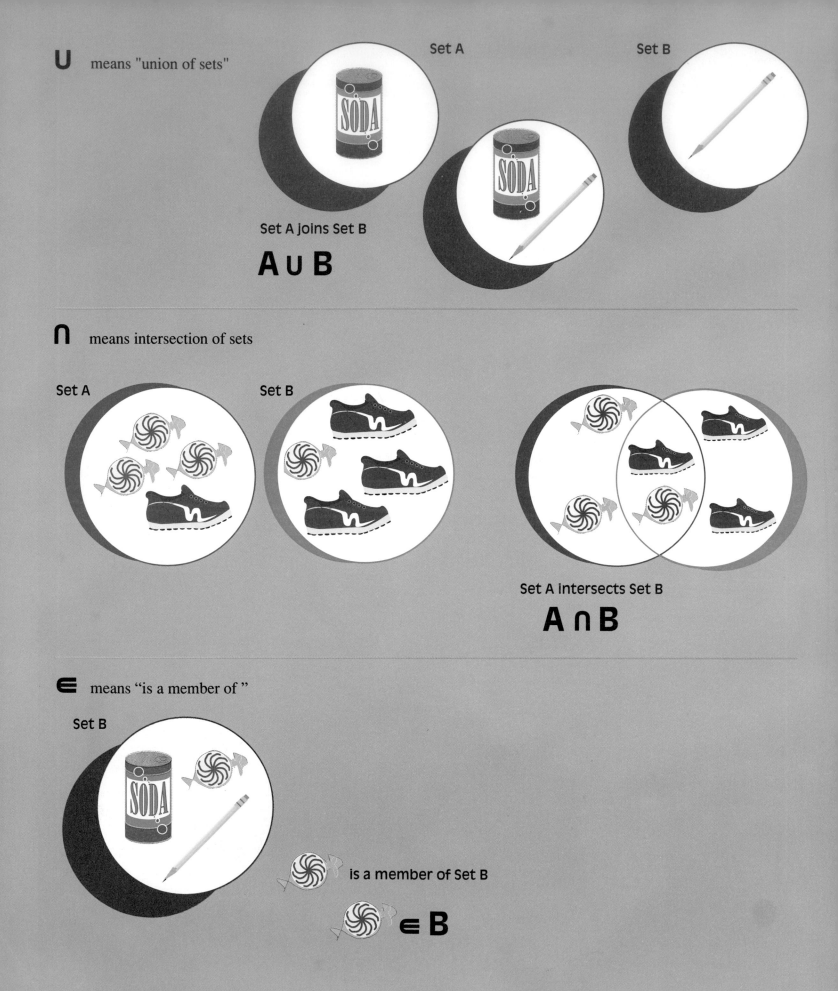

Set A

Set B

Set A joins Set B

A ∪ B

∩ means intersection of sets

Set A

Set B

Set A intersects Set B

A ∩ B

∈ means "is a member of "

Set B

is a member of Set B

∈ B

⊂ means "is a proper subset of"

Set C

Set D

If all the members of Set D are also members of Set C, but Set C has more members,

D ⊂ C.

⊆ means "is equal to and a subset of"

Set E

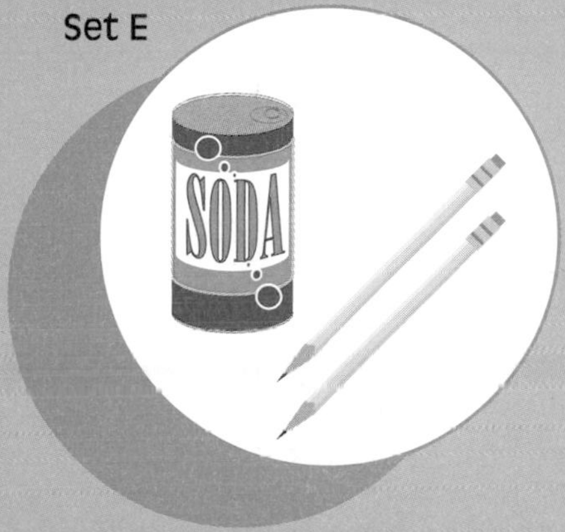

Set F

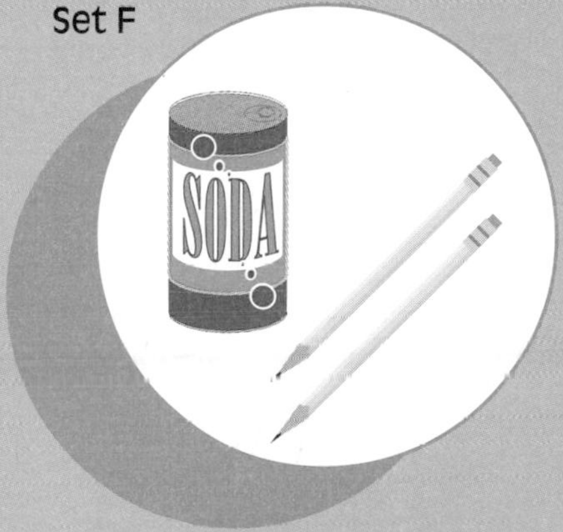

If Set E and Set F are identical sets, **E ⊆ F** and **F ⊆ E.**

{ } or Ø means "empty set" or a set with no members

▶ *An empty set is a subset of any set.*
All sets are subsets of themselves.

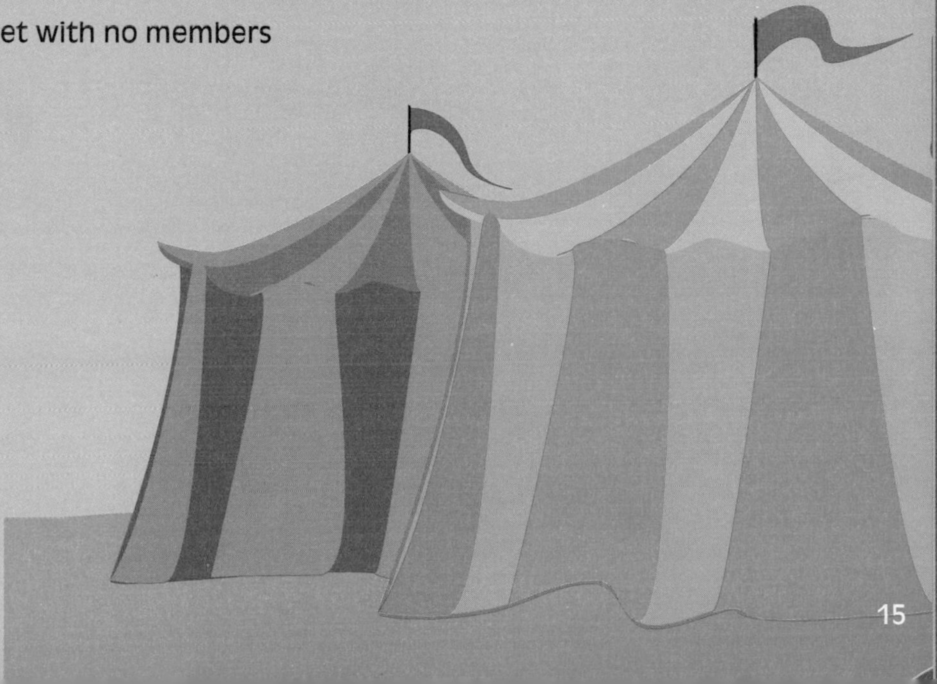

Place Value

In the decimal, or base 10, system, numbers are grouped by tens. That means that there are only ten different numerals used to make up decimal numbers:

0, 1, 2, 3, 4, 5, 6, 7, 8, and **9**

After these ten numerals are used separately, they are combined to stand for more numbers.

0	1	2	3	4	5	6	7	8	9
10	11	12	13	14	15	16	17	18	19
20	21	22	23	24	25	26	27	28	29
30	31	32	33	34	35	36	37	38	39
40	41	42	43	44	45	46	47	48	49
50	51	52	53	54	55	56	57	58	59
60	61	62	63	64	65	66	67	68	69
70	71	72	73	74	75	76	77	78	79
80	81	82	83	84	85	86	87	88	89
90	91	92	93	94	95	96	97	98	99
100	101	102	103	104	105	106	107	108	109...

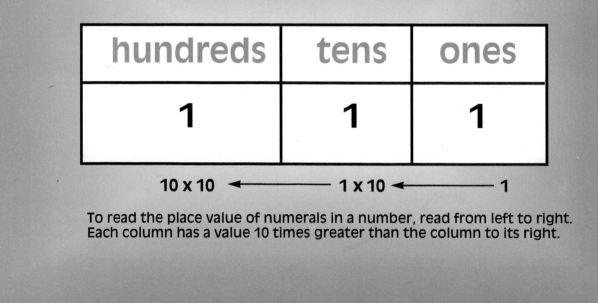

Number: 111

In the number *111*, each numeral *1* means a different number: *one*, *ten*, and *one hundred*. How can the numeral *1* stand for so many numbers? That's called *place value*. The *value* of a numeral depends on what *place* it's in. If our number system didn't use place value, we would need a lot more than ten numerals—we'd need millions!

hundreds	tens	ones
1	1	1

10 x 10 ◄——— 1 x 10 ◄——— 1

To read the place value of numerals in a number, read from left to right. Each column has a value 10 times greater than the column to its right.

See also Decimals and Place Value, p. 44.

Periods

Three places in the place value chart make up a *period*. Periods are always counted from the right—from the "ones" column—of a number. Periods are separated in numerals by commas.

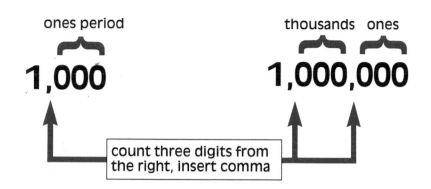

ones period

1,000

thousands ones

1,000,000

count three digits from the right, insert comma

Millions Period			Thousands Period			Ones Period		
Hundred Millions	Ten Millions	Millions	Hundred Thousands	Ten Thousands	Thousands	Hundreds	Tens	Ones
100,000,000	10,000,000	1,000,000	100,000	10,000	1,000	100	10	1
900,000,000	90,000,000	9,000,000	900,000	90,000	9,000	900	90	9

Place Holder

The numeral *0* is called the *place holder*.

thousands	hundreds	tens	ones
		1	0
	2	0	0
3	0	0	0

If one **0** is added to the right of **1**, it means 10 ones, or **10**.

If two **0s** are added to the right of **2**, it means 2 hundreds, or **200**.

If three **0s** are added to the right of **3**, it means 3 thousands, or **3,000**.

Order

Ordering numbers means listing numbers from least to greatest, or from greatest to least. Two symbols are used in ordering.

<   is less than

>   is greater

Sometimes numbers in a set can be *"greater than or equal to"* members of another set. Likewise, members of a set are sometimes *"less than or equal to"* members of another set. A bar is added to *less than* and *greater than* symbols to show they are also equal.

≤   is less than or equal to

≥   is greater than or equal to

Number lines show numbers in order. If you follow the number line to the right, the numbers get larger and larger. If you follow the number line to the left, the numbers get smaller and smaller.

numbers become larger ⟶

⟵ −1   0   1   2   3   4   5 ⟶

⟵ numbers become smaller

Order can also be shown on a pie chart.

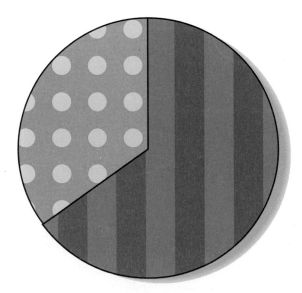

The striped area is greater than the polka dot area.

Base 2

Base 2, or the binary system, uses only two numerals, *0* and *1*, to represent all the numbers to infinity. Base 2 has place values like base 10, and they look like this:

Base 5

Base 5 uses five numerals: *0*, *1*, *2*, *3*, and *4*. Like base 2, these numerals are combined to represent numbers to infinity. Base 5's place values look like this:

Decimal (Base 10)	Base 2					Place Value / Base 10 Equivalent	Base 5			
	2^4	2^3	2^2	2^1	2^0		5^3	5^2	5^1	5^0
	16	8	4	2	1		125	25	5	1
0	0	0	0	0	0		0	0	0	0
1	0	0	0	0	1		0	0	0	1
2	0	0	0	1	0		0	0	0	2
3	0	0	0	1	1		0	0	0	3
4	0	0	1	0	0		0	0	0	4
5	0	0	1	0	1		0	0	1	0
6	0	0	1	1	0		0	0	1	1
7	0	0	1	1	1		0	0	1	2
8	0	1	0	0	0		0	0	1	3
9	0	1	0	0	1		0	0	1	4
10	0	1	0	1	0		0	0	2	0
...	...	...	...	...	...		...	...	...	...
15	0	1	1	1	1		0	0	3	0
16	1	0	0	0	0		0	0	3	1
...	...	...	...	...	...		...	...	...	...
20	1	0	1	0	0		0	0	4	0

See also Powers and Exponents, p 24.

Converting Base 10 to Base 2

To change 22 in base 10 to base 2, find the greatest equivalent place value. Look on the conversion chart. It's **20,** or **10100** in base 2. Then continue to find the equivalent value for **2,** or **00010**. Add the columns to find the base 10 / base 2 equivalent.

Base 10		Base 2	
20	or	**10100**	— Find the greatest equivalent place value.
+ 2	or	**00010**	— Find the remaining equivalent place values.
22		**10110**	— Add columns to find base 10 / base 2 equivalent.

Converting Base 10 to Base 5

To change 18 in base 10 to base 5, find the greatest equivalent place value. It's **16,** or **31** in base 5. Then find the remaining equivalent value. Add the columns to find the base 10 / base 5 equivalent.

Base 10		Base 5	
16	or	**31**	— Find the greatest equivalent place value.
+ 2	or	**+ 02**	— Find the remaining equivalent place values.
18		**33**	— Add columns to find base 10 / base 5 equivalent.

Square, Triangular, and Rectangular Numbers

Square numbers

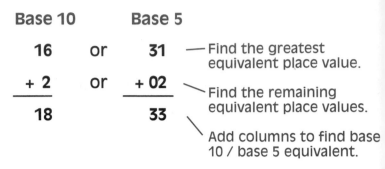

| 1 | 4 | 9 | 16 |

Triangular numbers

| 1 | 3 | 6 | 10 |

Rectangular numbers

| 1 | 6 | 8 | 12 |

Expanded Notation

When you write a number with more than one digit, the placement of each digit determines its value (see Place Value, p. 16). Look at 12 and 21:

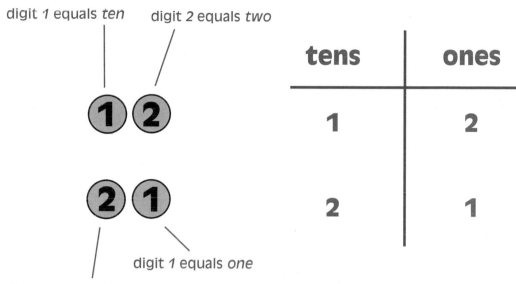

digit *1* equals *ten*   digit *2* equals *two*

tens	ones
1	2
2	1

digit *2* equals *twenty*   digit *1* equals *one*

Using the digits *1* and *2*, you can make the numbers *12* and *21*.

When you write the number **twelve** in numeral form, you ordinarily write **12**. This way of writing a number is known as **standard notation**. But there is another way to write the number twelve.

10 + 2

Or still another way.

(1 x 10) + 2

These spread out, or "expanded" ways of writing **12** are called **expanded notation**. You can describe any number using expanded notation. Take a look at the number **six hundred fifty-four thousand, three hundred twenty-one**. In standard notation, this number is written **654,321**. In expanded notation, it can be written several ways:

600,000 + 50,000 + 4,000 + 300 + 20 + 1 = 654,321

or

(6 x 100,000) + (5 x 10,000) + (4 x 1,000) + (3 x 100) + (2 x 10) + (1 x 1) = 654,321

or

$$6 \times 10^5 + 5 \times 10^4 + 4 \times 10^3 + 3 \times 10^2 + 2 \times 10^1 + 1 = 654{,}321$$

Factors and Multiples

Factors

Factors are two numbers that, when multiplied together, form a new number called a **product** (see Multiplication, p. 33). For example, *1* and *2* are factors of *2*, and *3* and *4* are factors of *12*.

Every number except *1* has at least two factors: *1* and itself.

Composite numbers have more than two factors. In fact, every composite number (see p. 8) can be written as the product of prime numbers. You can see this on a **factor tree**.

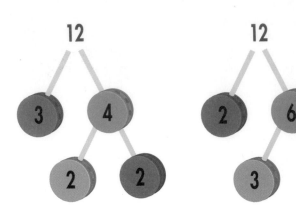

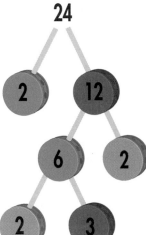

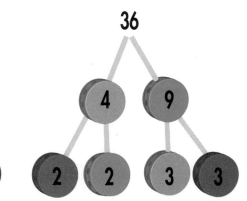

The Greatest Common Factor

Common factors are numbers that are factors of two or more numbers. For example, *2* is a factor of *12* and *36*, which makes *2* a common factor of *12* and *36*. The common factor of two numbers with the greatest value is called the **greatest common factor**. For example, *2, 3, 4, 6,* and *12* are common factors of *12* and *36*, but *12* is the greatest common factor.

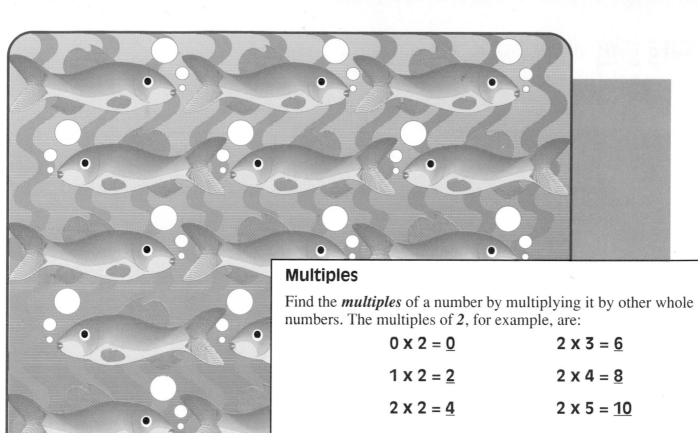

Multiples

Find the *multiples* of a number by multiplying it by other whole numbers. The multiples of *2*, for example, are:

0 x 2 = <u>0</u>	2 x 3 = <u>6</u>
1 x 2 = <u>2</u>	2 x 4 = <u>8</u>
2 x 2 = <u>4</u>	2 x 5 = <u>10</u>

. . . and so on.

As you can see, the multiples of *2* include *0*, *2*, *4*, *6*, *8*, and *10*. The list continues into infinity!

Common Multiples, 0 – 5

Some numbers share the same multiples. Those multiples are known as *common multiples*.

Number	Multiples					
0	0	0	0	0	0	0
1	0	1	2	3	4	5
2	0	2	4	6	8	10
3	0	3	6	9	12	15
4	0	4	8	12	16	20
5	0	5	10	15	20	25
	0	1	2	3	4	5

The least multiple of two or more numbers is the least common multiple. For example, the least common multiple of *2* and *3* is *6*.

2 x 1 = 2	2 x 2 = 4	2 x 3 = **6**
3 x 1 = 3	3 x 2 = **6**	

Powers and Exponents

To find the *powers* of a number, multiply the number over and over by itself. The *first power* is the number. The *second power* is the product of the number multiplied once by itself. The *third power* is the number multiplied twice by itself, and so on. For example:

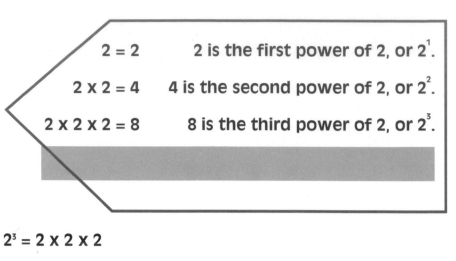

$$2 = 2 \qquad \text{2 is the first power of 2, or } 2^1.$$

$$2 \times 2 = 4 \qquad \text{4 is the second power of 2, or } 2^2.$$

$$2 \times 2 \times 2 = 8 \qquad \text{8 is the third power of 2, or } 2^3.$$

$$2^1 = 2 \times 1 \qquad 2^2 = 2 \times 2 \qquad 2^3 = 2 \times 2 \times 2$$

$$3^1 = 3 \times 1 \qquad 3^2 = 3 \times 3 \qquad 3^3 = 3 \times 3 \times 3$$

 There is a special way of writing the power of a number called an **exponent.** *It's the tiny number written above and to the right of the number.*

	1	2	3	4	5	6	7	8	9
first power	$1^1 = 1$	$2^1 = 2$	$3^1 = 3$	$4^1 = 4$	$5^1 = 5$	$6^1 = 6$	$7^1 = 7$	$8^1 = 8$	$9^1 = 9$
second power (squared)	$1^2 = 1$	$2^2 = 4$	$3^2 = 9$	$4^2 = 16$	$5^2 = 25$	$6^2 = 36$	$7^2 = 49$	$8^2 = 64$	$9^2 = 81$
third power (cubed)	$1^3 = 1$	$2^3 = 8$	$3^3 = 27$	$4^3 = 64$	$5^3 = 125$	$6^3 = 216$	$7^3 = 343$	$8^3 = 512$	$9^3 = 729$
tenth power	$1^{10} = 1$	$2^{10} = 2{,}018$	$3^{10} = 59{,}056$	$4^{10} = 1{,}048{,}576$	$5^{10} = 9{,}765{,}625$	$6^{10} = 60{,}466{,}176$	$7^{10} = 282{,}175{,}249$	$8^{10} = 1{,}075{,}741{,}824$	$9^{10} = 3{,}486{,}784{,}401$

Exponents

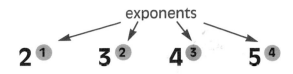

exponents

2^1 3^2 4^3 5^4

▶ *Is there a zero power? Yes. Any number, positive or negative, raised to the zero power is equal to 1.*

Palindromes semordnilaP

You've probably heard of palindromes in language—words and phrases that are the same read forward or backward.

mom

dad

noon

level

radar

Madam, I'm Adam

Able was I ere I saw Elba.

A man. A plan. A canal: Panama!

Rats live on no evil star.

There are number palindromes, too. For example:

22

101

2002

45654

You can create your own number palindromes using addition.

First pick a number:

245

Then, reverse its digits to create a new number:

542

Next, add the two numbers

245
+542
787

You've created a number palindrome!

Sometimes you'll have to keep reversing and adding to create the palindrome.

67
+76
143
+341
484

Squares and Square Roots

Raising a number to the second power is also called *squaring* a number. For example, *3 squared* (3^2) is equal to *9*, and the *square root* of *9* is *3*.

There is a special way to write the symbol for a square root called a *radical sign* $\sqrt{}$.

2 squared: 2^2 = 2 x 2 = 4

3 squared: 3^2 = 3 x 3 = 9

4 squared: 4^2 = 4 x 4 = 16

Square root of 16: $\sqrt{16}$ = 4

Square root of 9: $\sqrt{9}$ = 3

Square root of 4: $\sqrt{4}$ = 2

Table of Square Roots to 40

$\sqrt{1}$	1	$\sqrt{121}$	11	$\sqrt{441}$	21	$\sqrt{961}$	31
$\sqrt{4}$	2	$\sqrt{124}$	12	$\sqrt{484}$	22	$\sqrt{1,024}$	32
$\sqrt{9}$	3	$\sqrt{169}$	13	$\sqrt{529}$	23	$\sqrt{1,089}$	33
$\sqrt{16}$	4	$\sqrt{196}$	14	$\sqrt{576}$	24	$\sqrt{1,156}$	34
$\sqrt{25}$	5	$\sqrt{225}$	15	$\sqrt{625}$	25	$\sqrt{1,225}$	35
$\sqrt{36}$	6	$\sqrt{256}$	16	$\sqrt{676}$	26	$\sqrt{1,296}$	36
$\sqrt{49}$	7	$\sqrt{289}$	17	$\sqrt{729}$	27	$\sqrt{1,369}$	37
$\sqrt{64}$	8	$\sqrt{324}$	18	$\sqrt{784}$	28	$\sqrt{1,444}$	38
$\sqrt{81}$	9	$\sqrt{361}$	19	$\sqrt{841}$	29	$\sqrt{1,521}$	39
$\sqrt{100}$	10	$\sqrt{400}$	20	$\sqrt{900}$	30	$\sqrt{1,600}$	40

WHY A SQUARE?

We say that *5 squared* equals *25*, and that *25* is a *square number*. Why? Because *25* is the area of a square in which each side equals *5* (see p. 72).

BASIC MATH FUNCTIONS

1 Math *Symbols*

In math, the numerals *0, 1, 2, 3, 4, 5, 6, 7, 8,* and *9* stand for number values. A numeral, then, is a symbol that stands for a number.

Numerals aren't the only symbols used in math. Other symbols are used to show how numbers relate to each other. The addition sign, **+**, for example, is a symbol that stands for "plus." The subtraction sign, **−**, is a symbol that stands for "minus."

So, if you see *3 + 2*, you know *2* will be added together with *3*. And if you see *3 − 2*, you know *2* will be subtracted from *3*.

Basic Math Symbols

+	plus, add	**≥**	is greater than or equal to
−	minus, subtract	**≤**	is less than or equal to
X	multiplied by, multiply	**:**	is compared to, ratio
÷	divided by, divide	**∞**	infinity
=	equal to	**∠**	angle
≠	not equal to	**∟**	right angle
>	is greater than	**⊥**	perpendicular
<	is less than	**‖**	parallel to
Ø or **{ }** empty set		**√**	square root

2 Addition and Subtraction

Combining two or more numbers is called **addition**. The term for addition is **plus**, and the symbol for plus is **+**. The numbers that are combined in addition are called **addends** and together they form a new number called a **sum**.

"Taking away" one or more numbers from another number is called **subtraction**. The term for subtraction is **minus**, and the symbol for minus is **−**. The number being subtracted is called a **subtrahend**. The number being subtracted from is called a **minuend**. The new number left after subtracting is called a **remainder** or **difference**.

The complete addition or subtraction "sentence" is called an **equation**. An equation has two parts. The two parts are separated by the **equal sign**, **=**. For example, **the minuend minus the subtrahend equals the difference.** An **addition fact** or a **subtraction fact** is the name given to specific addition and subtraction equations.

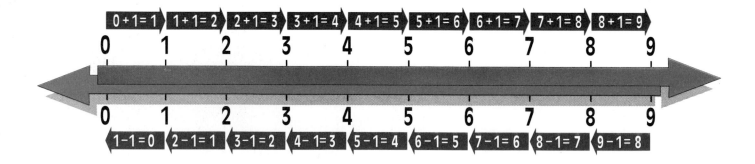

Carrying Numbers

Addition often produces sums with a value greater than **9** in a given place (see Place Value, p. 16). The value over ten is then **carried** to the next place.

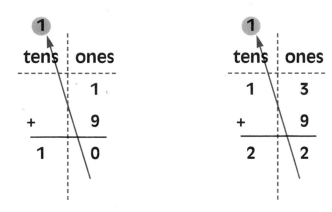

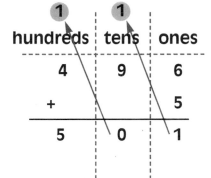

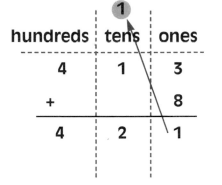

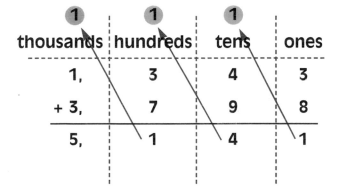

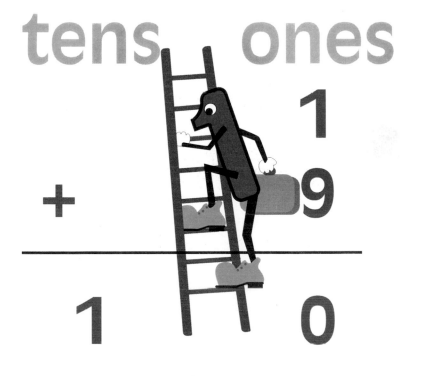

Borrowing or Exchanging

Borrowing, sometimes called *exchanging*, means "borrowing" a ten to make a number large enough to complete subtraction in one row of numerals. Borrowing is necessary only in the subtraction of numbers greater than *10* or in subtracting decimal fractions (see p. 44) .

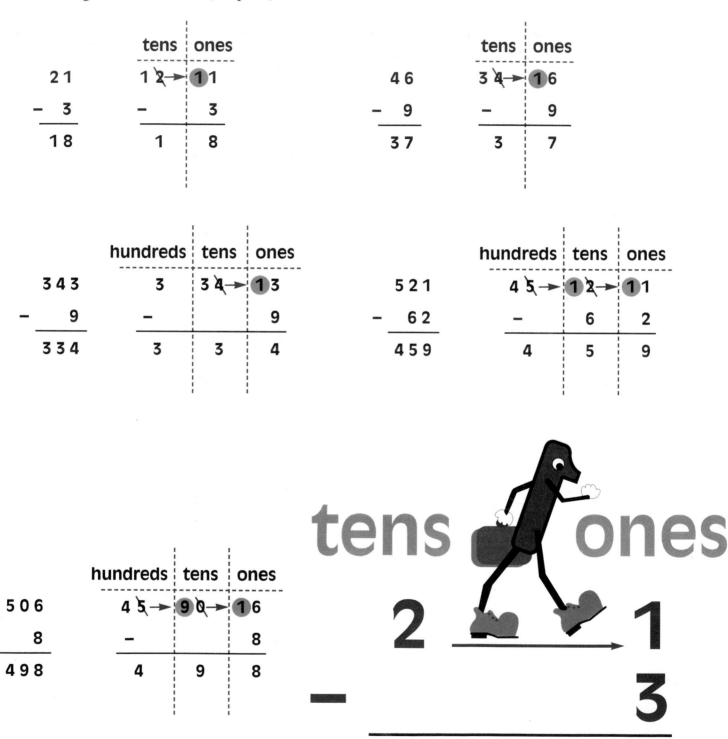

Adding and Subtracting Whole Numbers

Adding whole numbers is as simple as 2 + 2! To add two whole numbers, you can simply follow the number line and complete the addition fact.

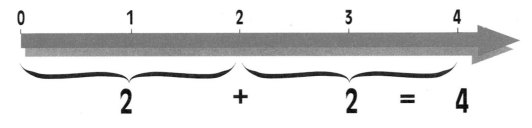

2 + 2 = 4

Table of Addition Facts

+	1	2	3	4	5	6	7	8	9	10
1	2	3	4	5	6	7	8	9	10	11
2	3	4	5	6	7	8	9	10	11	12
3	4	5	6	7	8	9	10	11	12	13
4	5	6	7	8	9	10	11	12	13	14
5	6	7	8	9	10	11	12	13	14	15
6	7	8	9	10	11	12	13	14	15	16
7	8	9	10	11	12	13	14	15	16	17
8	9	10	11	12	13	14	15	16	17	18
9	10	11	12	13	14	15	16	17	18	19
10	11	12	13	14	15	16	17	18	19	20

The **SUM** Is Always the **SAME**

Pick a three-digit number with the first digit larger than the last by at least two. Then reverse the numerals in the number you've picked and subtract this new number from the original number. Compute the remainder. Next, reverse the numerals in the remainder, and add this new number to the remainder. The sum will equal 1,089—no matter what number you started with!

$$\begin{array}{r} 543 \\ - 345 \\ \hline 198 \\ + 891 \\ \hline 1{,}089 \end{array}$$

reverse digits, then subtract from original number

reverse digits, then add to remainder

$$\begin{array}{r} 614 \\ - 416 \\ \hline 198 \\ + 891 \\ \hline 1{,}089 \end{array}$$

Adding and Subtracting Integers

Adding and subtracting positive integers works the same way as adding and subtracting whole numbers. Adding and subtracting negative numbers works differently.

When you add a negative integer to a positive integer, you are actually subtracting the value of the negative integer from the positive integer.

$4 + {}^-2 = 4 - 2 = 2$

$7 + 3 + {}^-2 = 7 + 3 - 2 = 8$

$11 + {}^-6 + 4 + {}^-2 = 11 - 6 + 4 - 2 = 7$

When you add a negative integer to another negative integer, you add the values of the integers and then add a negative sign in front of them.

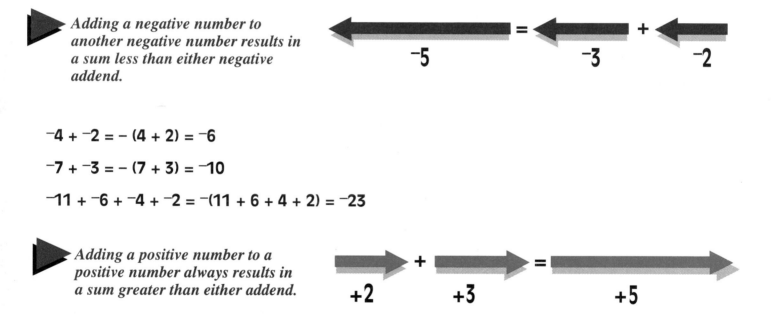

Adding a negative number to another negative number results in a sum less than either negative addend.

$^-4 + {}^-2 = - (4 + 2) = {}^-6$

$^-7 + {}^-3 = - (7 + 3) = {}^-10$

$^-11 + {}^-6 + {}^-4 + {}^-2 = {}^-(11 + 6 + 4 + 2) = {}^-23$

Adding a positive number to a positive number always results in a sum greater than either addend.

When you subtract a negative integer from a negative integer, you are actually adding a positive integer to the negative integer.

$^-4 - {}^-2 = {}^-4 + 2 = {}^-2$

$^-7 - {}^-3 - {}^-2 = {}^-7 + 3 + 2 = {}^-2$

$^-11 - {}^-6 - {}^-4 - {}^-2 = {}^-11 + 6 + 4 + 2 = 1$

When you subtract a positive integer of greater value from another positive integer, the difference will be a negative integer.

$2 - 4 = {}^-2$

$3 - 7 - 2 = {}^-6$

$11 - 6 - 4 - 2 = {}^-1$

3 Multiplication and Division

Multiplication

What Is Multiplication?

Multiplication is a quick form of addition. By multiplying numbers together, you are really adding a series of one number to itself. For example, you can add *2* plus *2*. You can also multiply *2* times *2*. Both *2 plus 2* and *2 times 2* equal *4*.

$$2 + 2 = 4$$
$$2 \times 2 = 4$$

$$\begin{array}{cc} 2 & 2 \\ +2 & \times 2 \\ \hline 4 & 4 \end{array}$$

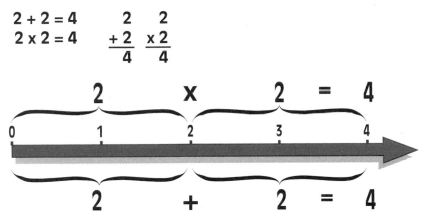

But what if you wanted to calculate the number of days in five weeks? You could add *7* days + *7* days + *7* days + *7* days + *7* days or you could multiply *7* days times *5*. Either way you arrive at *35*, the number of days in five weeks.

$$7 + 7 + 7 + 7 + 7 = 35$$
$$5 \times 7 \qquad\qquad = 35$$

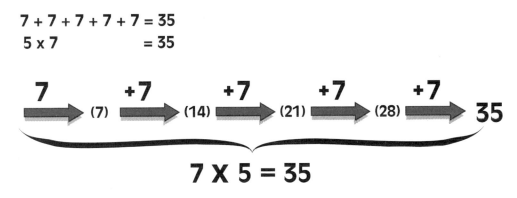

Although multiplication is related to addition, the parts of multiplication are not known as addends. Instead, the parts are known as *multiplicands* and *multipliers*. A multiplication sentence, like an addition sentence, is called an *equation*. But a multiplication sentence results in a *product*, not a sum.

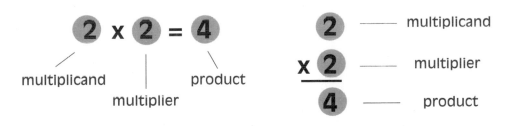

33

Multiplication Table

X	0	1	2	3	4	5	6	7	8	9	10	11	12
1	0	1	2	3	4	5	6	7	8	9	10	11	12
2	0	2	4	6	8	10	12	14	16	18	20	22	24
3	0	3	6	9	12	15	18	21	24	27	30	33	36
4	0	4	8	12	16	20	24	28	32	36	40	44	48
5	0	5	10	15	20	25	30	35	40	45	50	55	60
6	0	6	12	18	24	30	36	42	48	54	60	66	72
7	0	7	14	21	28	35	42	49	56	63	70	77	84
8	0	8	16	24	32	40	48	56	64	72	80	88	96
9	0	9	18	27	36	45	54	63	72	81	90	99	108
10	0	10	20	30	40	50	60	70	80	90	100	110	120
11	0	11	22	33	44	55	66	77	88	99	110	121	132
12	0	12	24	36	48	60	72	84	96	108	120	132	144

Multiplication, Step-by-Step

When the multiplicand and the multiplier are numbers with two or more digits, multiplication becomes a step-by-step process.

Look at 15 x 13:

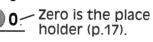

First, multiply the ones — 3 x 5. Line up the product with the ones column.

Next, multiply the tens — 3 x 1. Line up the product with tens column.

Zero is the place holder (p.17).

Last, add the ones and tens to find the product of the equation.

Here is a shorter way:

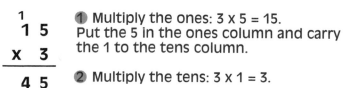

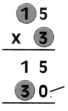

1️⃣ Multiply the ones: 3 x 5 = 15. Put the 5 in the ones column and carry the 1 to the tens column.

2️⃣ Multiply the tens: 3 x 1 = 3.

3️⃣ Add the 1 that you carried over to the 3, put the sum in the tens column.

Look at 265 x 23:

```
  2 6 5        First, multiply the
x   2 3        multiplicand by the
              ones in the
    1 5        multiplier — 3 x 5,
  1 9 0        3 x 6, and 3 x 2.
  6 0 0        Zero is the place
              holder (p. 17).
```

```
  2 6 5        Next, multiply by
x   2 3        the tens — 2 x 5, 2 x
              6, and 2 x 2. Zero is
    1 5        the place holder.
  1 9 0
  6 0 0
  1 0 0
1,2 0 0
4,0 0 0
```

```
    2 6 5    Last, add.
  x   2 3
      1 5
  +   1 9 0
  +   6 0 0
  +   1 0 0
  + 1,2 0 0
  + 4,0 0 0
    6,0 9 5
```

Here is the shorter way:

```
  11
  11
    265
x    23
    795

  5300
  6,095
```

① Multiply the ones: 3 x 265
   3 x 5 = 15 carry the 1
   3 x 6 = 18 plus the carried 1 = 19; carry the 1
   3 x 2 =   6 plus the carried 1 = 7.

② Multiply the tens: 2 x 265
   0 is the place holder
   2 x 5 = 10 carry the 1
   2 x 6 = 12 plus the carried 1 = 13; carry the 1
   2 x 2 = 4 plus the carried 1 = 5

③ Add 795 + 5300 = 6,095

Division

What Is Division?

Division is the process of finding out how many times one number, the *divisor*, will fit into another number, the *dividend*. The division sentence results in a *quotient*. The signs of division are ÷ and ‾|, and mean *divided by*. You can think of division as a series of repeated subtractions. For example, *40 ÷ 10* could also be solved by subtracting *10* from *40* four times:

40 − 10 − 10 − 10 − 10 = 0

Because *10* can be subtracted four times, you can say that *40* can be divided by *10* four times, or *40 ÷ 10 = 4*.

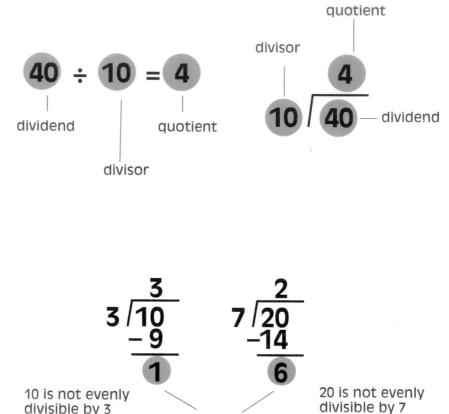

Many numbers do not fit evenly into other numbers. They are *not evenly divisible by* those numbers, and the number left over is called the *remainder*.

10 is not evenly divisible by 3

remainder

20 is not evenly divisible by 7

Division, Step-by-Step

Where the dividend and divisor are numbers with two or more digits, division becomes a step-by-step process.

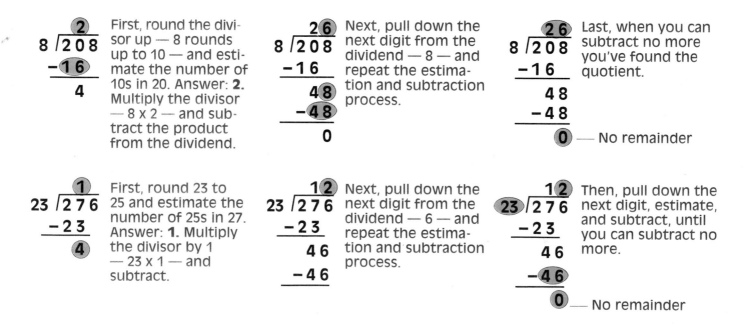

First, round the divisor up — 8 rounds up to 10 — and estimate the number of 10s in 20. Answer: **2.** Multiply the divisor — 8 x 2 — and subtract the product from the dividend.

Next, pull down the next digit from the dividend — 8 — and repeat the estimation and subtraction process.

Last, when you can subtract no more you've found the quotient.

— No remainder

First, round 23 to 25 and estimate the number of 25s in 27. Answer: **1.** Multiply the divisor by 1 — 23 x 1 — and subtract.

Next, pull down the next digit from the dividend — 6 — and repeat the estimation and subtraction process.

Then, pull down the next digit, estimate, and subtract, until you can subtract no more.

— No remainder

Whole Numbers

When you multiply whole numbers, the *product* usually has a greater value than either the *multiplicand* or the *multiplier*.

But there are exceptions:

A number multiplied by *1* is always equal to itself.

$$\begin{array}{r} 1 \\ \times\,1 \\ \hline 1 \end{array} \qquad 21 \times 1 = 21 \qquad \begin{array}{r} 36 \\ \times\,1 \\ \hline 36 \end{array} \qquad \frac{-1}{2} \times 1 = \frac{-1}{2}$$

A number multiplied by *0* is always equal to *0*.

$$\begin{array}{r} 1 \\ \times\,0 \\ \hline 0 \end{array} \qquad 21 \times 0 = 0 \qquad \begin{array}{r} 36 \\ \times\,0 \\ \hline 0 \end{array} \qquad \frac{-1}{2} \times 0 = 0$$

To divide whole numbers, reverse the process of multiplication. For example, if *2 x 7 = 14* in a multiplication equation, then in a division sentence, *14* is the *dividend* and *7* is the *divisor* in a division sentence with a *quotient* of *2*.

A whole number divided by *1* will always equal itself.

$$1 \div 1 = 1 \qquad 1\overline{)21}^{\,21} \qquad 36 \div 1 = 36 \qquad \frac{-1}{2} \div 1 = \frac{-1}{2}$$

Zero divided by a whole number will always equal *0*.

$$0 \div 12 = 0 \qquad 3\overline{)0}^{\,0} \qquad 0 \div \frac{-1}{2} = 0 \qquad \frac{0}{7} = 0$$

A number cannot be divided by *0*. The answer is *undefined*.

$$12 \div 0 = \text{undefined} \qquad 0\overline{)3}^{\,\text{undefined}} \qquad \frac{-1}{2} \div 0 = \text{undefined} \qquad \frac{7}{0} = \text{undefined}$$

Integers

Multiplying integers works the same way as multiplying whole numbers, unless one or more of the integers is a negative number.

The product of a positive integer multiplied by another positive integer will always be a positive integer. Positive integers may or may not be written with a positive sign: +8 = 8.

$$4 \times 2 = 8 \qquad \begin{array}{r} 3 \\ \times\, 2 \\ \hline 6 \end{array} \qquad \begin{array}{r} 7 \\ \times\, 1 \\ \hline 7 \end{array} \qquad \frac{1}{2} \times 3 = \frac{3}{2}$$

The product of a positive integer multiplied by a negative integer will always be a negative integer.

$$4 \times {}^{-}2 = {}^{-}8 \qquad \begin{array}{r} 3 \\ \times\, {}^{-}2 \\ \hline {}^{-}6 \end{array} \qquad \begin{array}{r} 7 \\ \times\, {}^{-}1 \\ \hline {}^{-}7 \end{array} \qquad \frac{1}{2} \times {}^{-}3 = \frac{{}^{-}3}{2}$$

The product of a negative integer multiplied by a positive integer will always be a negative integer.

$${}^{-}4 \times 2 = {}^{-}8 \qquad \begin{array}{r} {}^{-}3 \\ \times\, 2 \\ \hline {}^{-}6 \end{array} \qquad \begin{array}{r} {}^{-}7 \\ \times\, 1 \\ \hline {}^{-}7 \end{array} \qquad \frac{{}^{-}1}{2} \times 3 = \frac{{}^{-}3}{2}$$

The product of a negative integer multiplied by a negative integer will always be a positive integer.

$${}^{-}4 \times {}^{-}2 = 8 \qquad \begin{array}{r} {}^{-}3 \\ \times\, {}^{-}2 \\ \hline 6 \end{array} \qquad \begin{array}{r} {}^{-}7 \\ \times\, {}^{-}1 \\ \hline 7 \end{array} \qquad \frac{{}^{-}1}{2} \times {}^{-}3 = \frac{3}{2}$$

 Remember:
positive x positive = positive
positive x negative = negative
negative x positive = negative
negative x negative = positive

4 Fractions

The word *fraction* means "part of a whole." The word comes from the Latin word *fractio*, meaning "broken into pieces." In math, a fraction means one or more parts of a whole or a set.

A necklace is made up of beads. Each bead is a member of the "set," or necklace. Since 17 beads make up this necklace, each bead is 1/17 of the necklace.

A fraction has two parts, a *denominator* and a *numerator*. The denominator is the number written under the bar and tells the number of parts a whole is divided into. The numerator is the number written above the bar. The numerator tells the number of parts of the whole that are being counted.

$$\frac{\text{numerator}}{\text{denominator}} \qquad \frac{\text{number of parts counted}}{\text{total parts of the whole or set}} \qquad \frac{1}{17}$$

 A fraction is another way of writing a division problem. The fraction 1/4 means 1 ÷ 4. The denominator of a fraction can never be 0 because you cannot divide numbers by 0 (see p. 37).

Proper Fractions

When the numerator of a fraction is smaller than the denominator, the fraction is called a *proper fraction*.

$$\frac{1}{2} \qquad \frac{2}{5} \qquad \frac{3}{8} \qquad \frac{4}{9} \qquad \frac{5}{11}$$

 The value of a proper fraction is always less than one.

Improper Fractions

When the numerator of a fraction is larger than or equal to the denominator, the fraction is called an *improper fraction*.

$$\frac{3}{2} \qquad \frac{4}{3} \qquad \frac{5}{4} \qquad \frac{6}{5} \qquad \frac{7}{6} \qquad \frac{8}{8}$$

▶ *The value of an improper fraction is always greater than or equal to one.*

Mixed Numerals

Mixed numerals combine whole numbers and fractions. The values of mixed numerals can also be written as *improper fractions*. To write a mixed numeral as an improper fraction, multiply the whole number by the denominator of the fraction, then add the numerator. Use your answer as the new numerator and keep the original denominator.

$$1\frac{1}{2} = \frac{(2 \times 1) + 1}{2} = \frac{3}{2} \qquad\qquad 2\frac{3}{4} = \frac{(2 \times 4) + 3}{4} = \frac{11}{4}$$

To change an improper fraction to a mixed numeral, divide the numerator by the denominator. Then place the remainder over the old denominator.

$$\frac{3}{2} = 2\overline{\smash{\big)}\,3} = 1\frac{1}{2} \qquad\qquad \frac{11}{4} = 4\overline{\smash{\big)}\,11} = 2\frac{3}{4}$$
$$\underline{-2} \qquad\qquad\qquad \underline{-8}$$
$$1 \qquad\qquad\qquad\qquad\quad 3$$

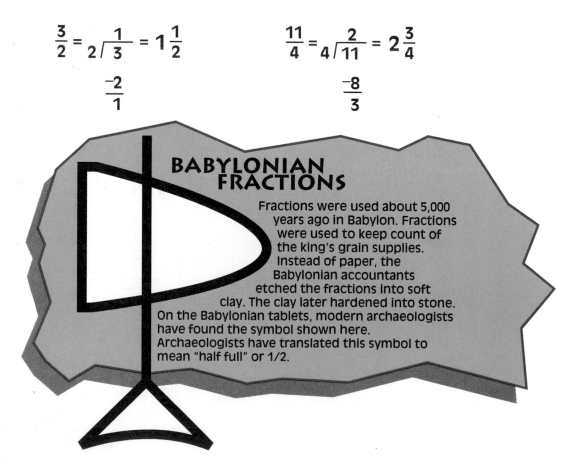

BABYLONIAN FRACTIONS

Fractions were used about 5,000 years ago in Babylon. Fractions were used to keep count of the king's grain supplies. Instead of paper, the Babylonian accountants etched the fractions into soft clay. The clay later hardened into stone. On the Babylonian tablets, modern archaeologists have found the symbol shown here. Archaeologists have translated this symbol to mean "half full" or 1/2.

Common Denominators

Many fractions have **common denominators**. That means that the numbers in their denominators are the same.

$$\frac{1}{2} \qquad \frac{3}{2} \qquad \frac{5}{2}$$

To find common denominators, ① find the **least common multiple** (see p. 23) for the denominators of the fractions you are comparing. Compare:

$$\frac{1}{2} \quad \text{and} \quad \frac{2}{3} \qquad \text{Answer: least common multiple is 6}$$

② Divide the value of the common multiple by the denominators.

$$2\overline{)\,6\,}^{\,3} \qquad 3\overline{)\,6\,}^{\,2}$$

③ Then multiply the quotients by the old numerators to calculate the new numerators.

$$\begin{array}{c}3\\ \times 1\\ \hline 3\end{array} \qquad \begin{array}{c}2\\ \times 2\\ \hline 4\end{array}$$

④ Place the new numerators over the common denominator.

$$\frac{3}{6} \qquad \frac{4}{6}$$

Adding and Subtracting Fractions

To add fractions, the fractions must have **common denominators**. To add fractions with common denominators, simply add the numerators. The sum will become the numerator of your answer. The denominator will remain the same.

$$\frac{1}{3} + \frac{4}{3} = \frac{1+4}{3} = \frac{5}{3}$$

To subtract fractions, you must also find the common denominator. Then subtract the numerators to find the remainder. The denominator will remain the same.

$$\frac{7}{8} - \frac{5}{8} = \frac{7-5}{8} = \frac{2}{8}$$

To add and subtract mixed numerals, rewrite the numerals as improper fractions. Then follow the process outlined above.

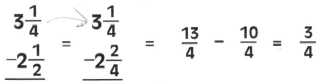

$$\begin{array}{c}3\frac{1}{4}\\ -2\frac{1}{2}\end{array} = \begin{array}{c}3\frac{1}{4}\\ -2\frac{2}{4}\end{array} = \frac{13}{4} - \frac{10}{4} = \frac{3}{4}$$

▶ *Adding and subtracting fractions is impossible without first writing the fractions with common denominators.*

Equivalent Fractions

A napkin is folded into two parts. One part is yellow, the other red.

$$\frac{1}{2} \quad \text{yellow}$$
$$\frac{1}{2} \quad \text{red}$$

Then the napkin is folded again. Now there are two yellow parts and two red parts.

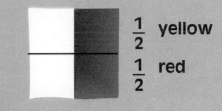

$$\frac{1}{2} \quad \text{yellow}$$
$$\frac{1}{2} \quad \text{red}$$

In this example, the red part of the napkin can be described as ½ red or ¾ red. That makes ½ and ¾ **equivalent fractions.**

When solving math problems, reduce fractions to their lowest equivalent. Rather than describing the napkin as ¾ yellow, call it ½ yellow.

Some Equivalent Fractions

$$\frac{1}{2} = \frac{2}{4} = \frac{3}{6} = \frac{4}{8} = \frac{5}{10}$$

$$\frac{1}{4} = \frac{2}{8} = \frac{3}{12} = \frac{4}{16} = \frac{5}{20}$$

$$\frac{1}{3} = \frac{2}{6} = \frac{3}{9} = \frac{4}{12} = \frac{5}{15}$$

▶ *To reduce a fraction to its lowest terms, divide both the numerator and the denominator by their greatest common denominator.*

$$\frac{4}{8} \div \frac{4}{4} = \frac{1}{2}$$

Multiplying and Dividing Fractions

Multiplying

To multiply a fraction by a whole number, multiply the numerator by the whole number. The product becomes the numerator in the product fraction. The denominator will remain the same.

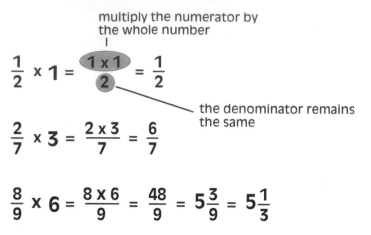

$$\frac{1}{2} \times 1 = \frac{1 \times 1}{2} = \frac{1}{2}$$

$$\frac{2}{7} \times 3 = \frac{2 \times 3}{7} = \frac{6}{7}$$

$$\frac{8}{9} \times 6 = \frac{8 \times 6}{9} = \frac{48}{9} = 5\frac{3}{9} = 5\frac{1}{3}$$

 Change improper fractions to mixed numerals. Be sure the fraction part of the mixed numeral is written in the lowest possible terms.

To multiply one fraction by another fraction, multiply the numerators. Their product will become the new numerator. Next, multiply the denominators. Their product will become the new denominator.

$$\frac{1}{2} \times \frac{1}{3} = \frac{1 \times 1}{2 \times 3} = \frac{1}{6}$$

$$\frac{7}{8} \times \frac{1}{3} = \frac{7}{24}$$

$$\frac{4}{3} \times \frac{1}{11} = \frac{4 \times 1}{3 \times 11} = \frac{4}{33}$$

To multiply mixed numerals (see p. 40) by fractions, change the mixed numerals to improper fractions. Then multiply the fractions.

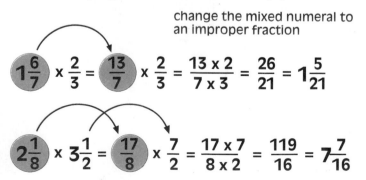

$$1\frac{6}{7} \times \frac{2}{3} = \frac{13}{7} \times \frac{2}{3} = \frac{13 \times 2}{7 \times 3} = \frac{26}{21} = 1\frac{5}{21}$$

$$2\frac{1}{8} \times 3\frac{1}{2} = \frac{17}{8} \times \frac{7}{2} = \frac{17 \times 7}{8 \times 2} = \frac{119}{16} = 7\frac{7}{16}$$

Dividing

To divide a fraction by a whole number, multiply the denominator of the fraction by the whole number. The quotient will be the new denominator. The numerator will remain the same.

numerator remains
the same

$$\frac{1}{2} \div 1 = \frac{①}{2 \times 1} = \frac{1}{2}$$

multiply the denominator
by the whole number

$$\frac{2}{7} \div 3 = \frac{2}{7 \times 3} = \frac{2}{21}$$

To divide a whole number by a fraction or to divide a fraction by another fraction, *invert* the divisor fraction. Then multiply the fractions.

$$\frac{1}{2} \div \frac{1}{3} = \frac{1}{2} \times \frac{3}{1} = \frac{1 \times 3}{2 \times 1} = \frac{3}{2} = 1\frac{1}{2}$$

$$7 \div \frac{6}{8} = 7 \times \frac{8}{6} = \frac{7 \times 8}{6} = \frac{56}{6} = 9\frac{2}{6} = 9\frac{1}{3}$$

invert the divisor fraction and multiply

To divide a mixed numeral by another mixed numeral, first change the mixed numerals to improper fractions.

$$4\frac{1}{2} \div 2\frac{1}{3} = \frac{9}{2} \div \frac{7}{3} = \frac{9}{2} \times \frac{3}{7} = \frac{27}{14} = 1\frac{13}{14}$$

$$7\frac{6}{8} \div 6\frac{1}{3} = \frac{62}{8} \div \frac{19}{3} = \frac{62}{8} \times \frac{3}{19} = \frac{186}{152} = 1\frac{34}{152}$$

Turn it Upside Down: Inverting

Inverting a fraction means turning it upside down, or reversing the numerator and the denominator.

$$\frac{1}{3} \text{ inverted is } \frac{3}{1} \qquad \frac{6}{8} \text{ inverted is } \frac{8}{6}$$

Inverting a whole number means to make it the denominator of a fraction with 1 as the numerator. 3 inverted is ⅓, 7 inverted is ⅐.
So, to solve the problem ⅓ ÷ 3,

$$\text{invert } 3 \text{ or } \frac{3}{1} \text{ to } \frac{1}{3}$$

$$\text{then } \frac{1}{3} \times \frac{1}{3} = \frac{1 \times 1}{3 \times 3} = \frac{1}{9}$$

Decimal Fractions and Decimal Numbers

Decimal fractions or *decimals* are fractions with denominators of *10* or powers of *10* (see Powers, p. 24).

10, 100, 1,000, 10,000, and so on

Decimal fractions are written using a decimal point

$$\frac{1}{10} = .1 \qquad \frac{1}{100} = .01 \qquad \frac{1}{1000} = .001$$

A fraction is written as a decimal fraction (or decimal) by eliminating the denominator and adding a decimal point as many places to the left of the numerator as there are zeroes in the denominator. For example:

$$\frac{25}{100} = 25 \div 100 = .25 \qquad\qquad \frac{6}{10} = 6 \div 10 = .6$$

Count over two places   Count over one place

Decimals and Place Value

	hundreds	tens	ones	Decimal point	tenths	hundredths	thousandths
$10\frac{1}{10}$		1	0	.	1		
$205\frac{3}{100}$	2	0	5	.	0	3	
$4\frac{9}{1000}$			4	.	0	0	9

Changing a Fraction to a Decimal

Any fraction can be written as a decimal by dividing the numerator by the denominator, and adding a decimal point in the correct place.

$$\frac{1}{10} = 10\overline{)\,1.0\,}^{.1} \qquad \frac{3}{5} = 5\overline{)\,3.0\,}^{.6} \qquad \frac{1}{4} = 4\overline{)\,1.00\,}^{.25}$$

Repeating Decimals

Some fractions, when written as a division sentence, never reach a final digit. For example:

$$\frac{1}{3} = 3\overline{)1.000}^{.33\overline{3}}$$
$$\frac{9}{}$$
$$\overline{10}$$
$$\frac{9}{}$$
$$\overline{10}$$

Here, the decimal .3333 . . . could go on forever! This type of decimal is called a *repeating decimal*, and is written with a bar above the repeating numeral, as shown in the example above.

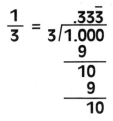

In decimal notation, a decimal point distinguishes whole numbers from decimal fractions:

$$1 = 1.0$$
$$\frac{1}{10} = 0.1$$
$$1\frac{1}{10} = 1.1$$

Decimal/ Fraction Equivalents

halves	fourths	eighths	sixteenths	thirty-seconds	sixty-fourths	decimal
					1	.015625
				1	2	.03125
					3	.046875
			1	2	4	.0625
					5	.078125
				3	6	.09375
					7	.109375
		1	2	4	8	.125
					9	.140625
				5	10	.15625
					11	.171875
*Example:			3	6	12	.1875
					13	.203125
				7	14	.21875
					15	.234375
1	2	4	8	16	32...	

halves	fourths	eighths	sixteenths	thirty-seconds	sixty-fourths	decimal
1	2	4	8	16	.25	
					17	.265625
				9	18	.28125
					19	.296875
			5	10	20	.3125
					21	.328125
				11	22	.34375
					23	.359375
		3	6	12	24	.375
					25	.390625
				13	26	.40625
					27	.421875
			7	14	28	.4375
				15	30	.46875
					31	.484375
1	2	4	8	16	32	.5
					33	.515625

Right table

halves	fourths	eighths	sixteenths	thirty-seconds	sixty-fourths	decimal
				17	34	.53125
					35	.546875
			9	18	36	.5625
					37	.578125
				19	38	.59375
					39	.609375
		5	10	20	40	.625
					41	.640625
				21	42	.65625
					43	.671875
			11	22	44	.6875
					45	.703125
				23	46	.71875
					47	.734375
	3	6	12	24	48	.75
					49	.765625
				25	50	.78125
					51	.796875
			13	26	52	.8125
					53	.828125
				27	54	.84375
					55	.859375
		7	14	28	56	.875
					57	.890625
				29	58	.90625
					59	.921875
			15	30	60	.9375
					61	.953125
				31	62	.96875
					63	.984375
2	4	8	16	32	64	1.

*Example: $\frac{3}{16} = \frac{6}{32} = \frac{12}{64} = .1875$

45

Computing with Decimals

Decimals have "common denominators" in the powers of *10*. (See Decimals and Place Value, p. 44.) So, adding and subtracting decimals is easy.

Adding and Subtracting Decimals

First, align the decimal points of the decimals. Then treat decimal fractions like whole numbers, aligning the decimal point in the sum or remainder. Adding and subtracting decimals may look familiar—it's just like adding and subtracting money (see Money, p. 109)!

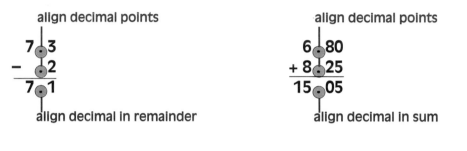

```
   align decimal points              align decimal points

      7.3                               6.80
    − .2                              + 8.25
      7.1                              15.05

   align decimal in remainder       align decimal in sum
```

Multiplying Decimals

To multiply decimals, treat them as if they were whole numbers, at first ignoring the decimal point.

```
    4.1
  x .3
  1 2 3
```

Next, count the number of places to the right of the decimal point in the multiplicand. Add this to the number of places to the right of the decimal point in the multiplier.

```
   4.①   multiplicand _____    one place
  x .③   multiplier  _____   + one place
                                   two places
```

Last, insert the decimal point in the product by counting over from the right the appropriate number of places.

```
    4.1
  x .3
  1,2 3   — count over two places from right
```
insert decimal point

Here are two other examples:

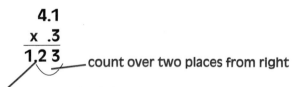

```
                              8.9            65.003
                            x 1.0          x .025
                              0 0          325015
                            8 9            130006
                            8. 9 0         1.625075
```

Dividing Decimals

Begin dividing decimals the same way you would divide whole numbers.

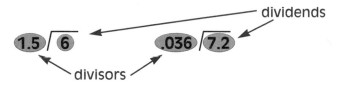

(Note that 6 = 6.0.)

Write the divisor as a whole number. Do this by multiplying the divisor by a power of *10* large enough to make it into a whole number.

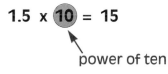

Then multiply the dividend by the same power of 10.

$$6 \times \boxed{10} = 60$$

Continue the division process as usual.

Align the decimal point in the remainder with the decimal point in the dividend.

Here is another example: $.036 \times \boxed{1,000} = 36$

$$7.2 \times \boxed{1,000} = 7,200$$

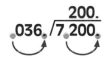

Ratios and Percentages

Ratios describe *proportion*. Proportion means the size of things in comparison to each other. When the numerator and the denominator of a fraction are compared, it can be called a *ratio*. Ratios are sometimes written in the form of fractions. More often, the symbol **:** is used to separate the numerator and the denominator.

For example, if you ate **2** parts of a pie that had been cut into **5** parts, the ratio of pieces of pie you ate to the total number of pieces of pie is $\frac{2}{5}$. The ratio **2:5** is the equivalent of the fraction $\frac{2}{5}$.

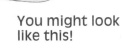

You might look like this!

If you ate 2/5 of a pie, the pie would look like this.

Percentages are ratios written as decimal fractions (see p. 44). The term *percent* means *one part in a hundred*. Any fraction with a denominator of *100* can be written as a percentage, using a percent sign, *%*. So, if you ate $\frac{2}{5}$ of a pie, you ate $\frac{40}{100}$ or *40%* of the pie.

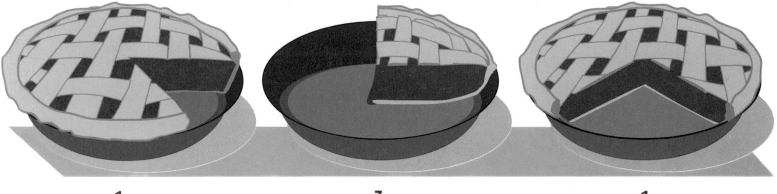

$\frac{1}{8}$ or 12.5% $\frac{3}{4}$ or 75% $\frac{1}{3}$ or 33.3%

Calculating Ratios and Percentages

Ratios

If you ate $\frac{2}{3}$ of a pie, how many *ninths* did you eat?

$$\frac{2}{3} = \frac{?}{9}$$

To find the answer, multiply the numerator of one fraction by the denominator of the other. The product will equal the product of the other numerator and denominator.

$$\frac{2}{3} \times \frac{?}{9} = 2 \times 9 = 3 \times ?$$

$$\frac{18}{3} = \frac{3 \times ?}{3}$$ Divide each side by 3.

$$6 = ?$$ The quotient is the missing number.

Answer: You ate $\frac{6}{9}$ of the pie.

▶ $\frac{2}{3}$ *and* $\frac{6}{9}$ *are* **equivalent ratios.**

Percentages

To change a fraction to a percent, divide the fraction.

$$\frac{2}{5} = 5\overline{)2.00}^{.40}$$

Then change the decimal to a fraction with **100** in the denominator, then to a percent.

$$.40 = \frac{40}{100} = 40\%$$

To change a percent to a fraction, reverse the process. Be sure to write the fraction in its lowest possible terms (see p. 41).

$$4\% = \frac{4}{100} = \frac{1}{25} \quad 13\% = \frac{13}{100}$$

To find a percent of a number, multiply the number by the percent written in its decimal fraction form. Find 25% of 12.

$$.25 \times 12 = 3$$

To find what percent one number is of another, divide the first number by the second, translate the number into its decimal fraction form, then into its percentage form. What percent of **12** is **48**?

$$\frac{12}{48} \text{ or } 48\overline{)12.00}^{.25} = 25\%$$

To find a number when a percent of it is known, calculate the ratios as shown above. Nine is **25%** of what number?

$$\frac{25}{100} = \frac{9}{?} \qquad 25 \times ? = 100 \times 9$$

$$\frac{25 \times ?}{25} = \frac{900}{25}$$

$$? = 36$$

5 Rounding Off and Estimation

What's Rounding Off?

Rounding off means to increase or decrease a number to equal a factor of ten. You can round numbers off to any factor of ten: to ones, tens, hundreds, thousands, ten thousands, and so on.

If you are rounding 3 to the nearest tens place, you would round down to 0, because 3 is closer to 0 than it is to 10.

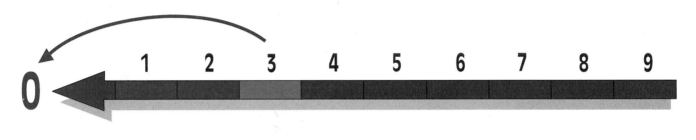

If you were rounding 9, you would round up to 10.

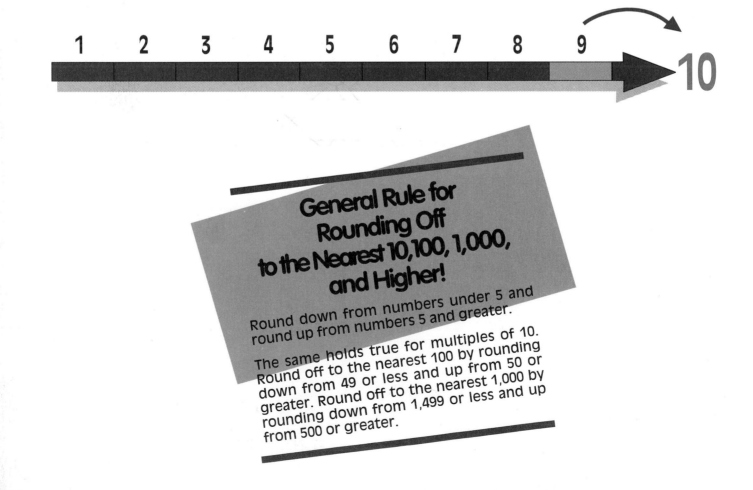

General Rule for Rounding Off to the Nearest 10, 100, 1,000, and Higher!

Round down from numbers under 5 and round up from numbers 5 and greater.

The same holds true for multiples of 10. Round off to the nearest 100 by rounding down from 49 or less and up from 50 or greater. Round off to the nearest 1,000 by rounding down from 1,499 or less and up from 500 or greater.

Why Round Off?

Sometimes you have to figure out a math problem without using a pencil and paper or a calculator. Rounding numbers makes them easier to work with. Check out the shopping lists. One list tells the prices of five items. The other list shows the same prices, rounded to the nearest ten cents. Which list is easier to add up in your head?

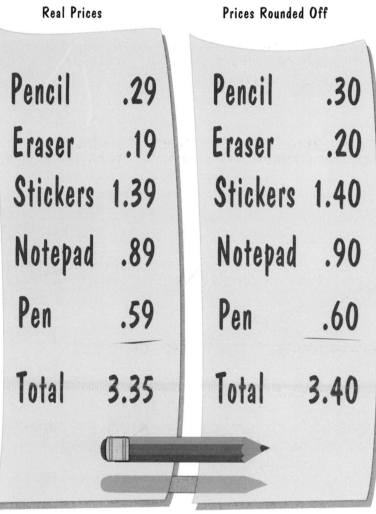

Real Prices	
Pencil	.29
Eraser	.19
Stickers	1.39
Notepad	.89
Pen	.59
Total	3.35

Prices Rounded Off	
Pencil	.30
Eraser	.20
Stickers	1.40
Notepad	.90
Pen	.60
Total	3.40

Estimation

To *estimate* means to make a good guess. Rounding off allows you to estimate more easily.
Here's one way to estimate the sum of **97 + 21**:

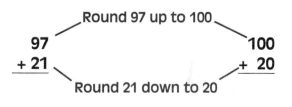

Round 97 up to 100

$$\begin{array}{r} 97 \\ + 21 \end{array} \qquad \begin{array}{r} 100 \\ + 20 \end{array}$$

Round 21 down to 20

$$\begin{array}{r} 97 \\ + 21 \end{array}$$

is about equal to 120

What about 129 – 11?

$$\begin{array}{r} 129 \\ - 11 \end{array} \longrightarrow \begin{array}{r} 130 \\ - 10 \end{array}$$

$$\begin{array}{r} 129 \\ - 11 \end{array}$$

is about equal to 120

6 Averages and Medians

Averages

The most common way to find an *average* is to add up a list of numbers and divide the sum by the number of items on the list. Another word for average is *mean*.

3 + 4 + 6 + 8 + 9 = 30

30 ÷ 5 = 6 So, the average is 6.

When do you need to calculate an average? Your grades may be based on the average of all your test scores. In sports, you might want to find out the average height of players on your favorite basketball team.

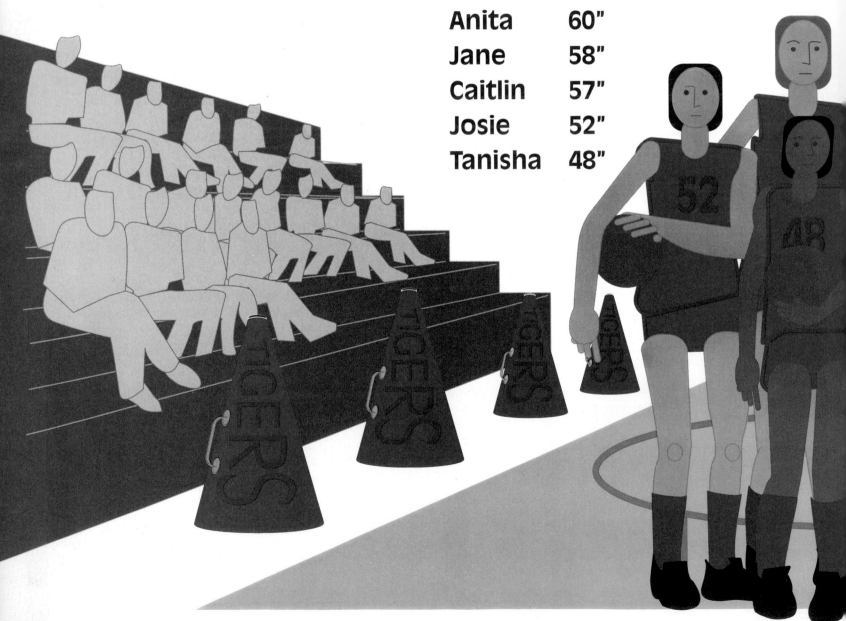

Anita	60"
Jane	58"
Caitlin	57"
Josie	52"
Tanisha	48"

Medians

Average or mean is different from *median.* The median is the middle number in a series of numbers stated in order from least to greatest. An average and a median can be the same number. The average of *3*, *5*, and *7* is *5*:

3 + 5 + 7 = 15 and 15 ÷ 3 = 5

and the median of *3*, *5,* and *7* is *5*. But average and median are often different numbers. Averages and medians are important in the branches of math called *probability* and *statistics* (see Statistics and Probability, pages 118–123).

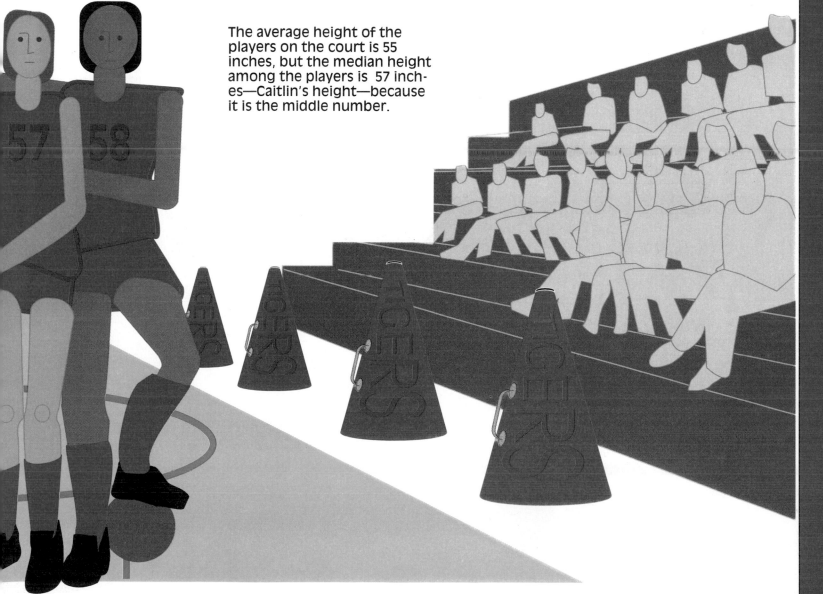

The average height of the players on the court is 55 inches, but the median height among the players is 57 inches—Caitlin's height—because it is the middle number.

7 Properties and Orders

Addition and multiplication fall under certain rules called *properties* or laws. Among the most important are the *commutative*, *associative*, and *distributive* properties.

Commutative Property

The commutative property of addition says that: *The sum of two or more numbers will always be the same, no matter in what order you add them.*

2 + 3 = 5 and **3 + 2 = 5**   **6 + 2 = 8** and **2 + 6 = 8**   **153 + 62 = 215** and **62 + 153 = 215**

The commutative property of multiplication says that: *The product of two or more numbers will always be the same, no matter in what order you multiply them*.

2 x 3 = 6 and **3 x 2 = 6**   **17 x 2 = 34** and **2 x 17 = 34**   **153 x 11 = 1,683** and **11 x 153 = 1,683**

Associative Property

The associative property of addition says that: *No matter how you group a series of numbers, they will always add up to the same sum.*

(1+ 2) + 3 = 6

1 + (2 + 3) = 6

(1 + 3) + 2 = 6

PARENTHESES IN PROBLEM SOLVING

Parentheses, (and), are used to group numbers together, especially in long math problems that combine addition, subtraction, multiplication, and division. There is a special order for solving long problems, called *order of operation* (see p. 55).

Parentheses help you group numbers to follow math properties and orders of operation.

1 + 2 + 3 + 4 + 5 =

(1 + 2) + (3 + 4) + 5 =

(3 + 7) + 5 =

10 + 5 =

15

Distributive Property

The distributive property says that: *Multiplication and addition can be linked together by "distributing" the multiplier over the addends in an equation.*

$$3 \times (1 + 4) = (3 \times 1) + (3 \times 4)$$

$$3 \times 5 = 3 + 12$$

$$15 = 15$$

Order of Operations

Sometimes the order in which you add, subtract, multiply, and divide is very important. For example, how would you solve the following problem?

$$2 \times 3 + 6$$

Would you group

$$(2 \times 3) + 6 \text{ or } 2 \times (3 + 6) ?$$

Which comes first, addition or multiplication? Does it matter?
Yes. Mathematicians have written two simple rules:

1. *Multiplication and division are carried out first, followed by addition and subtraction.* For example:

$$(2 \times 3) + 6 = 6 + 6 = 12 \text{ is correct}$$

$$2 \times (3 + 6) = 2 \times 9 = 18 \text{ is incorrect}$$

2. *When several numbers are to be multiplied or divided in the same equation, carry out the multiplication and division in the order they occur.* For example:

$$2 \times 3 - 7 \text{ is grouped } (2 \times 3) - 7 = 6 - 7 = {}^-1$$

3. *In a problem combining subtraction with addition or division with multiplication, carry out the processes in order from left to right:*

$$2 - 1 + 7 = (2 - 1) + 7 = 1 + 7 = 8$$

$$8 \div 2 \times 3 = (8 \div 2) \times 3 = 4 \times 3 = 12$$

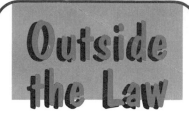

My Dear Aunt Sally,

To remember the order of operations, simply remember: Multiplication, Division, Addition, Subtraction or "*My Dear Aunt Sally*"

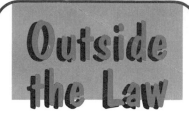

Outside the Law

The commutative and associative properties—or laws—are used *only* for addition and multiplication. *Subtraction and division are not commutative:*

$$1 - 2 \neq 2 - 1$$

$$-1 \neq 1$$

$$1 \div 2 \neq 2 \div 1$$

$$\frac{1}{2} \neq 2$$

And they are not associative:

$$(1 - 2) - 3 \neq 1 - (2 - 3)$$

$$-1 - 3 \neq 1 - -1$$

$$-4 \neq 0$$

$$(1 \div 2) \div 3 \neq 1 \div (2 \div 3)$$

$$\frac{1}{2} \div 3 \neq 1 \div \frac{2}{3}$$

$$\frac{1}{6} \neq \frac{3}{2}$$

You might say that subtraction and division are "outside the law!"

8 Story Problems

Clue Words

Within every story problem are several *clue words*. These words tell you the kind of math sentence to write to solve the problem.

Addition Clue Words

add
sum
total
plus
in all
both
together
increased by
all together

Subtraction Clue Words

subtract
difference
take away
less than
are not
remain
decreased by
have left
change (money problems)
how much more
fewer

Multiplication Clue Words

times
product of
multiplied by
by (dimension)

Division Clue Words

quotient of
divided by
half [or a fraction]
as much
split
separated
cut up
parts
sharing something equally

Multiplication clue words are also often the same as addition clue words. Multiply when you know both parts of the story problem and are asked to find "how many" or "how much."

Division clue words are often the same as subtraction clue words. Divide when you know the total and are asked to find the size or number of "one part" or "each part."

Writing Equations from Story Problems

1. Circle clue words.
2. Box important information.
3. Cross out unimportant information.

Mary has ten marbles. Lennie has thirteen. How many marbles do they have in all?

Mary has ten marbles . Lennie has thirteen . How many marbles do they have in all?

10 + 13 = _____

Fido has two treats in his bowl. He eats one. How many treats are left?

Fido has two treats in his bowl. He eats one . How many treats are left?

2 − 1 = _____

Ian has seven marbles. Kim has three times as many as Ian.
How many marbles does Kim have?

Ian has seven marbles . Kim has three times as many as Ian.
How many marbles does Kim have?

7 x 3 = _____

Mary and Lennie had twenty-three marbles together. They gave one marble to
Mustafa. Then Mary and Lennie divided the rest of their marbles into two equal parts.
How many marbles does Mary have now?

Mary and Lennie had twenty-three marbles together. They gave one marble to
Mustafa. Then Mary and Lennie divided the rest of their marbles into two equal parts.
How many marbles does Mary have now?

(23 − 1) ÷ 2 = _____

Strategies for Problem Solving

Simple Problems

In order to solve story problems, read the story, locate clue words and important information, and cross out unimportant information. Then come up with a strategy, or plan. Use the strategy to write an equation, or math sentence, to solve the story problem.

Mary has ten marbles. Lennie has thirteen. How many marbles do they have in all?

~~Mary has~~ ten marbles . ~~Lennie has~~ thirteen . How many marbles ~~do they have~~ in all?

10 + 13 = (23)

Fido has two treats in his bowl. He eats one. How many treats are left?

~~Fido has~~ two treats ~~in his bowl.~~ He ~~eats~~ one . How many treats are left?

2 − 1 = (1)

Ian has seven marbles. Kim has three times as many as Ian.

How many marbles does Kim have?

~~Ian has~~ seven marbles . ~~Kim has~~ three times ~~as many as Ian.~~

How many marbles ~~does~~ Kim have?

7 x 3 = (21)

Mary and Lennie had twenty-three marbles together. They gave one marble to Mustafa. Then Mary and Lennie divided the rest of their marbles into two equal parts. How many marbles does Mary have now?

~~Mary and Lennie had~~ twenty-three marbles ~~together.~~ They gave one ~~marble to~~ Mustafa. ~~Then Mary and Lennie~~ divided ~~the rest of their marbles~~ into two equal parts.

How many ~~marbles does Mary have now?~~

(23 − 1) ÷ 2 = (11)

Harder Problems

Some story problems are harder to solve than others. For some, you have to write two or three equations to solve the problem. For others, you may need to make charts or lists of information, draw pictures, find a pattern, or even guess and check. Sometimes you have to work backwards from a sum, product, difference, or quotient, or simply use your best logical thinking.

 Remember! Not all story problems can be solved in one step. Some require a strategy, or **plan**, *and may take several steps to solve.*

List/Chart

Marty's library book was six days overdue. The fine is $.05 the first day, $.10, the second, $.20 the third day, and so on. How much does Marty owe?

Marty's ~~library book~~ was six days overdue. ~~The fine~~ is $.05 the first day, $.10, the second, $.20 the third day, ~~and so on.~~ How much does Marty owe?

Answer: $1.60

DAYS	1	2	3	4	5	6
FINE	$.05	$.10	$.20	$.40	$.80	$1.60

Veronica, Archie, and Betty are standing in line to buy tickets to a concert. How many different ways can they order themselves in line?

Veronica, Archie, and Betty are standing in line to buy ~~tickets~~ to a ~~concert.~~ How many different ~~ways can they~~ order ~~themselves in line?~~

Veronica	Veronica	Archie	Archie	Betty	Betty
Archie	Betty	Veronica	Betty	Veronica	Archie
Betty	Archie	Betty	Veronica	Archie	Veronica

Answer: 6

Find a Pattern

Jenny's friend handed her a message in code and asked her to complete it. The message read 1, 2, 3 Z   4, 5, 6 Y   7, 8, 9 X_____. How did Jenny fill in the blanks?

Jenny's ~~friend handed~~ her a message in code and ~~asked her~~ to complete it.

The ~~message~~ read 1, 2, 3 Z   4, 5, 6 Y   7, 8, 9 X_____. How ~~did Jenny~~ fill in the blanks?

Answer: 10, 11, 12W

Draw a Picture

Mary is older than Jamie. Susan is older than Jamie, but younger than Mary. David is younger than Jamie. Who is oldest?

~~Mary~~ is older than ~~Jamie.~~ ~~Susan~~ is older than ~~Jamie,~~ but younger than ~~Mary.~~ ~~David~~ is younger than ~~Jamie.~~ Who is oldest?

Answer: Mary

Guess and Check

Farmer Joellen keeps cows and chickens in the farmyard. All together, Joellen can count 14 heads and 42 legs. How many cows and how many chickens does Joellen have in the farmyard?

~~Farmer Joellen~~ keeps cows and chickens in the ~~farmyard.~~ All together, ~~Joellen~~ can ~~count~~ 14 heads and 42 legs. How many cows and how many chickens ~~does~~ Joellen ~~have in the~~ farmyard?

6	cows
+8	chickens
14	heads

Guess a number of cows. Then add the number of chickens to arrive at the sum of 14 heads. Then check the total legs.

6 cows	= 24 legs
+8 chickens	= 16 legs
	40 legs

7	cows
+7	chickens
14	heads

Adjust your guesses. Then check again until you solve the problem.

7 cows	= 28 legs
+7 chickens	= 14 legs
	42 legs

Answer: 7 cows and 7 chickens

Work Backwards

Marsha was banker for the school play. She took in $175 in ticket sales. She gave Wendy $75 for sets and costumes and Paul $17.75 for advertising and publicity. After paying for the props, Marsha had $32.25 left. How much did the props cost?

Marsha was banker for the school play. She took in $175 in ticket sales. She gave Wendy $75 for sets and costumes and Paul $17.75 for advertising and publicity. After paying for the props, Marsha had $32.25 left. How much did the props cost?

$$
\begin{array}{ll}
\$\ 175.00 & \text{tickets} \\
-\quad 75.00 & \text{costumes} \\
\hline
\$\ 100.00 & \\
-\quad 17.75 & \text{advertising} \\
\hline
\$\quad 82.25 &
\end{array}
$$

$$
\begin{array}{ll}
\$\ 82.25 & \\
-\ 32.25 & \\
\hline
\$\ 50.00 & \text{cost of props}
\end{array}
$$

Logical Reasoning

Juan challenged Shelia to guess his grandmother's age in ten questions or less. It took her six. Here's what Shelia asked:

Juan challenged Shelia to guess his grandmother's age in ten questions or less. It took her six. Here's what Shelia asked:

"Is she less than fifty?" "No."	50 + years old
"Less than seventy-five?" "Yes."	50 to 75 years old
"Is her age an odd or even number?" "Odd."	
"Is the last number less than or equal to five?" "No."	odd number greater than 5, that ends in 7 or 9
"Is it nine?" "No."	ends in 7, 57 or 67
"Is she in her sixties?" "No."	57

MEASUREMENT

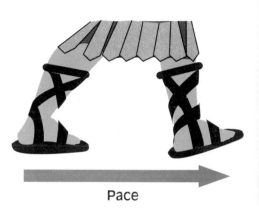

1 Measuring Length and Distance

A Short History

When people first began measuring, they didn't have rulers, so they used parts of their bodies as guides. For example, the *digit* was a measure based on the average width of an adult finger, about 3/4 of an inch.

Digit

Three grains of barley laid end to end equaled one *finger*, and the width of an outstretched adult hand from thumb to pinky tip was called a *span*.

Span

The ancient Egyptians used a measure called the *cubit*. The cubit was the average distance from the elbow to the tip of the middle finger of a grown man. The cubit is used as a measure in the Bible. Noah's Ark was about 300 cubits long. That's about 530 feet.

Cubit

The Egyptians also measured by *paces*. A pace was the distance covered in a single step or stride. The pace was stretched from the heel of the back foot to the big toe of the front foot. Although the pace isn't used for measuring today, we still use the term "pacing off" when we talk about dividing up an area.

Pace

The Egyptians had a name for a distance of 100 paces—the *stade*. Ancient Greeks called the stade a *stadion*. The Romans called the stade a *stadian*. The stadian was often used as a distance for foot races. From the words *stadion* and *stadian* comes our word *stadium*.

Fathom

The Vikings probably developed the **fathom**, a distance equal to the span of two outstretched arms. We still use fathoms today to measure the depths of seas and oceans.

The **hand** is another ancient unit of measurement. Today we use hands to measure the height of horses.

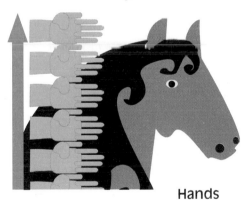

Hands

The Romans were the first to use the **foot** as a measure. The foot was equal to the length of a grown man's foot. Originally, the foot was divided into twelve **uncia**, or inches.

The Romans also created the **mile**. The mile was the distance covered by 1,000 **paces** of a Roman soldier, or about 5,280 feet.

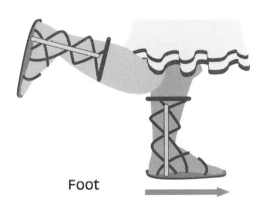

Foot

The Roman measurements—feet, inches, and miles—were picked up by the tribes of Britain. Over time, the measures were changed and some new measurements were created.

During the 1100s, the length of the British king's arm became known as the **yard**. The yard was about three Roman feet long.

Around this same time, the British wanted to make measurement more exact. Using body parts was no longer accurate enough, because two bodies are never exactly the same. So the British created a **standard length** from an iron bar. They called the bar the **standard yard**.

Copies of the standard yard were made for use all over the country. Soon the length of men's belts were measured from a standard yard of leather or rope.

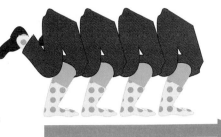

Rod

The British created another standard measure, the **rod**. The standard rod measured 16 1/2 feet. Before that, the rod was the length covered by the left feet of 16 men, lined up heel to toe.

Yard

The U.S. Customary and English Systems of Measuring Length

The *U.S. Customary System*, also called the *English System*, is our standard for measuring length. The system is a combination of a number of ancient measures. It is used along with the *metric system* (see next page).

U.S. Customary Measures of Length

Measure	Abbreviation	Equivalent
inch	in.	1/12 foot
foot	ft.	12 inches
yard	yd.	3 feet (36 inches)
rod	rd.	5 1/2 yards
furlong	fur.	40 rods (220 yards)
mile	mi.	1,760 yards (5,280 feet)
league		3 miles (5,280 yards)

Change larger to smaller units by multiplying

2 yards = ? inches

  2 x 36 (36 inches to a yard) = 72 inches

3 meters = ? cm

  3 x 100 (100 centimeters to a meter) = 300 centimeters

Change smaller to larger units by dividing

12 feet = ? yards

  12 ÷ 3 (3 feet to a yard) = 4 yards

5000 meters = ? km

  5000 ÷ 100 meters = 50 km

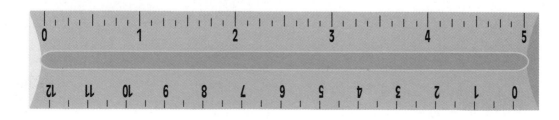

The Metric System for Measuring Length

In the 1790s, French scientists worked out a system of measurement based on the **meter**. The meter is one ten-millionth of the distance between the North Pole and the Equator. The French scientists made a metal rod equal to the length of the standard meter.

By the 1980s, the French metal bar was no longer a precise measure for the meter. Scientists figured out a new standard for the meter. They made it equal to $\frac{1}{299,792,548}$ of the distance light travels in a vacuum in one second. Since the speed of light in a vacuum never changes, the distance of the meter will not change.

Metric/U.S. Customary Length Equivalents

Metric Unit	Abbreviation*	Metric Equivalent	U.S. Equivalent
millimeter	mm	.1 centimeter	.04 inch
centimeter	cm	10 millimeters	.3937 inch
decimeter	dm	10 centimeters	3.937 inches
meter	m	100 centimeters	39.37 inches
dekameter	dcm	10 meters	32.81 feet (10.9 yards)
hectometer	hm	100 meters	109 yards
kilometer	km	1000 meters	1,093 yards (3,281 feet)

*Metric abbreviations usually have no periods.

Nautical Measures

Measurement at sea is different from measurement on land. Instead of using miles and kilometers, sailors favor *fathoms* and *nautical miles*.

Nautical Measures

Name	Measures	Equivalents
cable	distance	.1 nautical mile
degree	circular distance	60 nautical miles
fathom	depth	6 feet (1.83 meters)
knot	speed	1 nautical mile per hour
mark	depth	the depth measured on a plimsoll, or sounding line
nautical mile	distance	6,076 feet (1,857 meters)
marine league	distance	3.48 miles (5.6 kilometers)

Space Age Measures

Measuring Earth

More than 2,000 years ago, the ancient Greeks worked out a way to measure *circles* and *spheres*. They divided the circle into 360 parts, called *degrees.* The 360 degrees (360°) could also be used to divide spheres. Since the earth is roughly a sphere, the Greeks used degrees (360°) to measure it, too. The Greeks used vertical lines called *longitude* to mark off equal parts of the earth's surface. We still use lines of longitude today.

The line located at *0°* longitude is called the *prime meridian*. Distance is measured east and west of this line. Longitude lines east of the prime meridian are numbered *1°* through *179°*. Longitude lines west of the prime meridian are also numbered *1°* through *179°*. The *180°* line, reached by traveling east or west, is called the *International Date Line*.

The ancient Greeks also drew lines to divide up the earth north and south. These lines are called *lines of latitude*. Latitude is measured from the equator, or *0°*. Latitudes lines are numbered from the equator to the North Pole from *0°* through *90°*. Latitude lines are also numbered from *0°* through *90°* from the equator to the South Pole. Degrees of longitude and latitude are further divided into measures called *seconds*. Like minutes in an hour (see p. 85), there are 60 seconds in a degree of longitude or latitude.

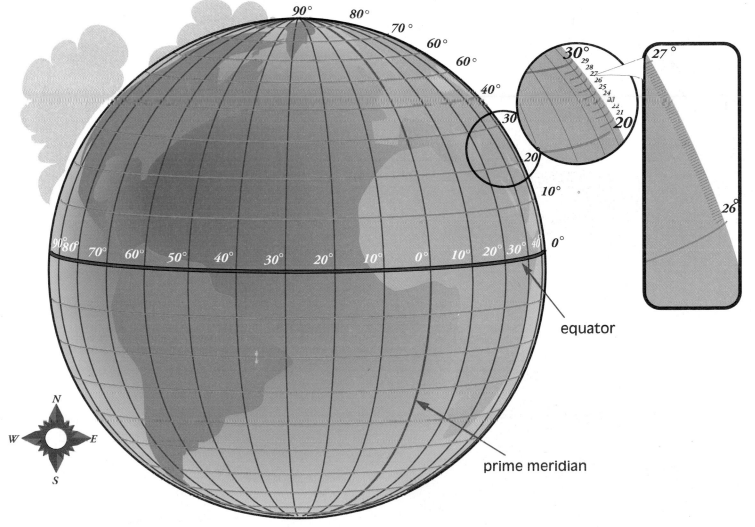

equator

prime meridian

Light Years

The distances in space are too great to be measured easily in miles or kilometers. Instead, scientists use *light years*. One light year is the distance light travels in one year. Light travels through space at a speed of 186,282 miles per second, so . . .

1 light year = 5.878 trillion miles = 9.5 trillion kilometers

Astronomers have also calculated a distance called a *parsec*.

1 parsec = 3.259 light years

Laser Ranging

Lasers are commonly used today, from grocery store scanning machines to surgical tools. They are also used for measuring distances in space.

In 1969, *Apollo* astronauts left a mirror on the moon. Laser beams bounced off this mirror, allowing us to measure the changes in the distance between the moon and earth. This technique, called *laser ranging* or LIDAR, is also helping scientists to measure the movements of the continents.

ASTRONOMICAL UNIT

Scientists created the *astronomical unit (AU)* to calculate distances within our solar system. The distance from earth to sun is 92.9 million miles, or *1* astronomical unit.

Distances of Planets from Sun in Astronomical Units

Mercury	.04 AU
Venus	.07 AU
Earth	1 AU
Mars	1.5 AU
Jupiter	5.2 AU
Saturn	9.6 AU
Uranus	19.2 AU
Neptune	30.1 AU
Pluto	39.4 AU

2 Measuring Weight

A Short History

More than 3,000 years ago, the Egyptians invented a scale made of a stick hung from a piece of rope. From the ends of the stick were hung two more ropes. Objects to be weighed were tied to one of the ropes hanging from the end of the stick. Standard weights were tied to the other end. Standard weights included the weight of bags of grain, stones, or seeds.

Egyptian Scale

The Weigh We Were

One of the earliest known measures of weight is the Babylonian *mina.* The mina weighed about 21 ounces, about a pound and a half. A five-mina weight was made out of metal and formed into the shape of a duck. A thirty-mina weight was formed into the shape of a swan. These weights were placed on scales and used mostly to measure grain.

Another early weight was the Greek *talent.* The talent weighed about 56.9 pounds. The *carat*, known then as the *karob*, meaning "little bean," was equal to the weight of four grains of wheat. Carats today equal 3.086 grains and are used to measure precious stones and metals (see Troy Weight, p. 70).

U.S. Customary and English Weights

In the United States, we use three different scales to measure weight: *Avoirdupois Weight*, *Troy Weight*, and *Apothecaries' Measures*.

Avoirdupois Weight

Avoirdupois weight is used to measure everything except precious metals and gemstones, and medicine.

1 grain (gr.) = 0.002285 ounces

1 dram (dr.) = 27 11/32 grains

1 ounce (oz.) = 16 drams, or 437.5 grains

1 pound (lb.) = 7,000 grains, or 16 ounces

1 hundredweight (cwt.) = 100 pounds

1 ton = 2,000 pounds, or 20 hundredweights

1 long hundredweight = 112 pounds

1 long ton, or gross = 2,240 pounds or 20 long hundredweights

Troy Weight

Troy weight is used to measure precious metals and gemstones.

1 grain (gr.) = 0.002083 ounces

1 carat (c.) = 3.086 grains

1 pennyweight (dwt.) = 24 grains

1 troy ounce (oz.t.) = 20 pennyweights, or 480 grains

1 troy pound (lb.t.) = 12 troy ounces, or 5,760 grains

Apothecaries' Measures

Apothecaries' measures are used to measure medicines. Apothecaries' measures are like troy weights, but they include some liquid measures as well as solid weights.

1 scruple = 20 grains

1 dram = 3 scruples, or 60 grains

1 apothecaries' ounce = 8 drams, or 480 grains

1 apothecaries' pound = 12 apothecaries' ounces, or 5,760 grains

1 minim or drop = 1/60 fluid dram, or 1/8 fluid ounce

Metric Weights

In the 1790s, French scientists devised the *metric* system. The system covered measurement of length (see p. 65), area, volume, and weight. The basic unit of weight in the metric system is the *gram*.

Metric and U.S. Customary Weight Equivalents

Metric	Abbreviation	Metric Equivalent	U.S. Customary Equivalent
gram	g	1,000 milligrams	.0353 ounce
milligram	mg	.001 gram	.0154 gram
centigram	cg	10 milligrams	.154 grains
decigram	dg	10 centigrams	1.5432 grains
decagram	dkg	10 grams	.353 ounce
hectogram	hg	100 grams	3.53 ounces
kilogram	kg	1,000 grams	2.204 pounds
metric ton	mt	1,000 kilograms	22,046.6 pounds (1.102 tons)

Why "Lb." for "Pound"?

The abbreviation *lb.* comes from the Latin *libra*, meaning a unit of weight equal to 1/125th of the *talent* (see p. 69), or one pound. When the English adopted the pound measure, they kept the Latin abbreviation.

3 Measuring Perimeter and Area

To measure flat spaces, like polygons (see p. 99), we calculate *perimeter* and *area*. Perimeter is the distance around a polygon. *Area* is the size of a flat surface in square units.

Calculating Perimeter

Perimeter is calculated in different ways, depending upon the shape of the surface. The perimeter of a surface outlined by straight lines is calculated by adding together the lengths of its sides.

25

26

26

25

25 + 26 + 25 + 26 = perimeter of the fence

The perimeter of a circle (see p. 103) is called *circumference*. Mathematicians calculate circumference with a special equation:

circumference = πd or 2πr

The equations are read *"circumference equals pi times diameter"* and *"circumference equals two times pi times radius."* **Diameter** is the length of a line drawn across the circle through its center. **Radius** is half of the diameter, or a line drawn from the center of a circle to any point on the circle.

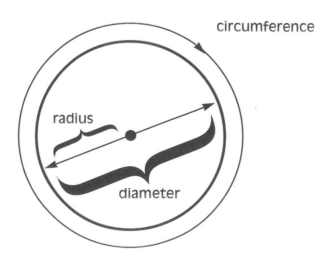

circumference

radius

diameter

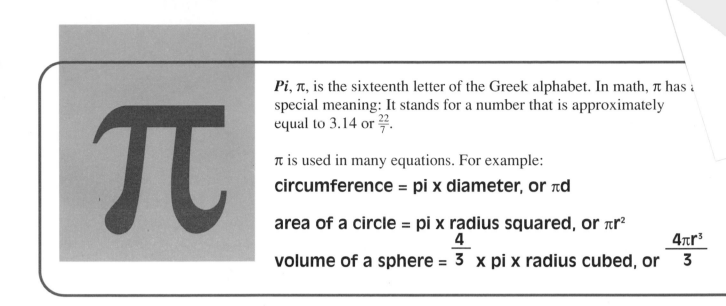

Pi, π, is the sixteenth letter of the Greek alphabet. In math, π has a special meaning: It stands for a number that is approximately equal to 3.14 or $\frac{22}{7}$.

π is used in many equations. For example:

circumference = pi x diameter, or πd

area of a circle = pi x radius squared, or πr²

volume of a sphere = $\frac{4}{3}$ x pi x radius cubed, or $\frac{4πr^3}{3}$

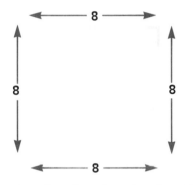

8 + 8 + 8 + 8 = 4 x 8 = 32
4s (4 sides) = perimeter
of a square

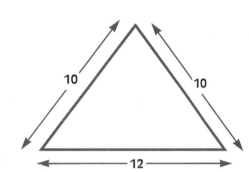

10 + 10 + 12 = 32
s + s + s = perimeter
of a triangle

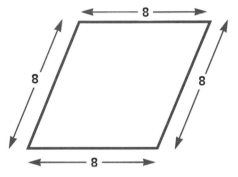

8 + 8 + 8 + 8 = 4 x 8 = 32
4s = perimeter of a
rhombus

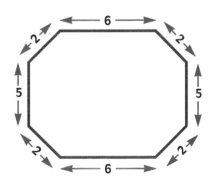

5 + 2 + 6 + 2 + 5 + 2 + 6 + 2 = 30
(Perimeter of an irregular
octagon)

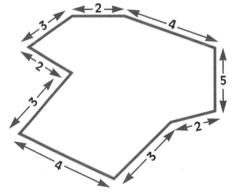

4 + 3 + 2 + 3 + 2 + 4 + 5 + 2 + 3 = 28
(Perimeter of an irregular
polygon)

~~ca~~lculating Area

Area, like perimeter, is calculated in different ways, depending on the shape of the surface.

An area with a perimeter made up of straight lines (see Polygons, p. 99) is calculated in different ways for different shapes:

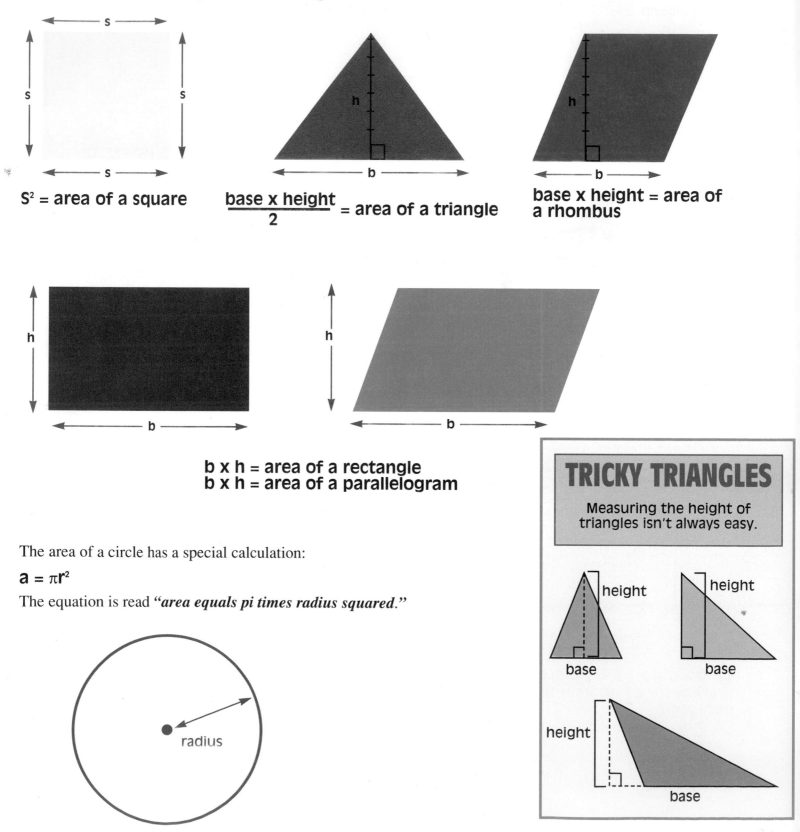

S^2 = **area of a square**

$$\frac{\text{base x height}}{2} = \text{area of a triangle}$$

base x height = area of a rhombus

b x h = area of a rectangle
b x h = area of a parallelogram

The area of a circle has a special calculation:

$$a = \pi r^2$$

The equation is read **"area equals pi times radius squared."**

radius

TRICKY TRIANGLES

Measuring the height of triangles isn't always easy.

height

height

base

base

height

base

Measuring Volume

Volume is the amount of space contained in a three-dimensional shape. Perimeter and area are measurements of only *two* dimensions, usually length and width (see pp. 72–74). Volume is a measurement of *three* dimensions, usually *length*, *width*, and *height*.

▶ *Liquids and gases can only be measured by volume. They have their own U.S. Customary and Metric measures (see p. 77).*

Calculating Volume

To find the volume of a *cube* or a *rectangular prism*, multiply length by width by height.

l x w x h = volume of rectangular prism

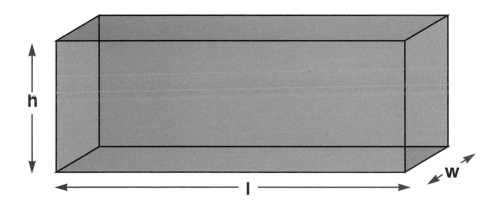

Since a cube has sides of equal length, multiply the length of one side by itself three times, s^3:

s^3 = volume of a cube

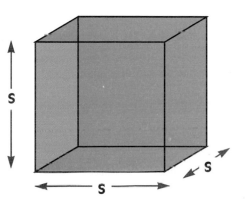

To find the volume of a *pyramid*, multiply the area of the base (B) by the height of the pyramid. Then divide the product by *3*.

$$\frac{B \times h}{3} = \text{volume of a pyramid}$$

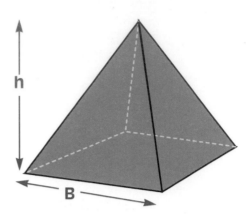

To find the volume of a *cylinder*, multiply the area of the base (B) or (πr^2) by the height of the cylinder.

$$B \times h =$$
volume of a cylinder
$$\pi r^2 \times h =$$

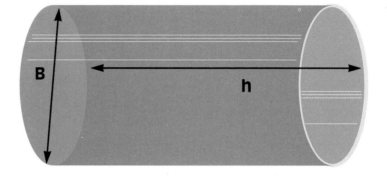

To find the volume of a *cone*, multiply the area of the base (B) or (πr^2) by the height of the cone. Then divide the product by *3*.

$$\frac{B \times h}{3} =$$
volume of a cone
$$\frac{\pi r^2 \times h}{3} =$$

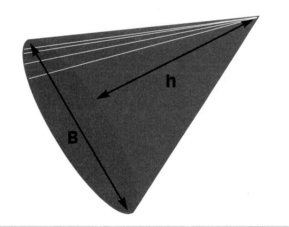

To calculate the volume of a *sphere*, multiply π by r^3. Then multiply the product by $\frac{4}{3}$.

$$\frac{4\pi r^3}{3} = \text{volume of a sphere}$$

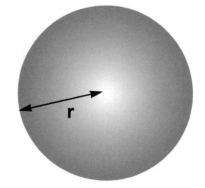

Metric and U.S. Customary Volume Equivalents

10 milliliters (mL)	=	1 centiliter (cL)		
10 centiliters	=	1 deciliter (dL)	=	100 milliliters
10 deciliters	=	1 liter (L)	=	1,000 milliliters
1 liter(s)	=	10 deciliter (dL)	=	100 centiliters
10 liters	=	1 dekaliter (daL)		
10 dekaliters	=	1 hectoliter (hL)	=	100 liters
10 hectoliters	=	1 kiloliter (kL)	=	1,000 liters

Liquid Measures

Measure	Abbreviation	Equivalent
gill	gi.	4 ounces
cup	c.	8 ounces
pint	pt.	2 cups
quart	qt.	2 pints
gallon	gal.	4 quarts
barrel	bar.	31.5 gallons

Cubic Measures

1,728 cubic inches	=	1 cubic foot
27 cubic feet	=	1 cubic yard
16 cubic feet	=	1 cord foot
8 cord feet	=	1 cord

5 Measuring Temperature

The Fahrenheit Scale

About 300 years ago, German physicist Gabriel Daniel Fahrenheit (1686-1736) invented a scale for measuring heat. His scale is still used today on thermometers, oven dials, water heaters, and thermostats.

Fahrenheit based his scale on the freezing and boiling points of water. On his scale, water freezes at 32°F and boils at 212°F. The 0°F mark was reached by mixing equal weights of snow (solid water) and salt. Of course, the "F" in the temperature readings stands for Fahrenheit!

The Centigrade Scale

In 1742, Swedish astronomer Anders Celsius (1701-1744) invented another scale for measuring heat. His scale is called the *centigrade* or *Celsius* scale. Like Fahrenheit's scale, Celsius's scale is based on the freezing and boiling points of water. Unlike the Fahrenheit scale, the freezing point of water is equal to 0°C. The boiling point is 100°C. While the Fahrenheit scale is used in the United States, the centigrade scale is used in most countries throughout the world. It is the scale preferred by scientists.

To convert from Fahrenheit to centigrade, subtract 32° from the Fahrenheit temperature and multiply the difference by 5. Then divide the product by 9.

$$\frac{5(F-32)}{9}$$

To convert centigrade to Fahrenheit, multiply the centigrade temperature by 9, divide the product by 5, and add 32°:

$$\frac{(C \times 9)}{5} + 32$$

Fahrenheit Scale

centigrade Scale

Fahrenheit/Centigrade Equivalents

°F	°C		°C	°F
0	−17.8		⁻50	⁻58
10	−12.2		0	32
20	⁻6.67		10	50
32	0		20	68
40	4.44		30	86
50	10		40	104
100	37.78		50	122
212	100		100	212

Absolute Zero

William Thompson, Lord Kelvin (1824–1907), devised a scale based on a very low temperature called **absolute zero**. The 0° mark on the Kelvin scale is equal to -459° on the Fahrenheit scale or -273° on the centigrade scale!

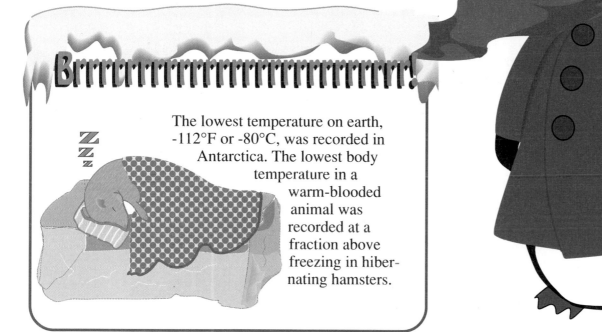

The lowest temperature on earth, -112°F or -80°C, was recorded in Antarctica. The lowest body temperature in a warm-blooded animal was recorded at a fraction above freezing in hibernating hamsters.

Hot Stuff!

Fahrenheit and centigrade scales are often used to measure body temperature. A healthy body temperature is around 98.6° F or 37°C.

But where does body heat come from?

What Is a Calorie?

Body heat comes primarily from eating food. The heat is measured in calories and **Kilocalories,** or 1,000 calories. A calorie is a metric measure. It stands for the amount of heat needed to raise the temperature of **1** gram of water **1** degree centigrade. By measuring the Kilocalories in the foods we eat, we can tell how much heat we can generate, or how many Kilocalories we can "burn" in daily activities (Kilocalories are often called Calories, with a capital **C**).

Calories and Your Body Weight

On days when you eat fewer Calories than the number of Calories you burn doing activities, you will burn Calories stored in the fat and muscles in your body. On days when you eat more Calories than you burn through activities, your body will store the excess Calories in the form of fat. So, when you eat too little, your body burns up fat. You might even lose weight. When you eat too much, your body stores Calories as fat. You might even gain weight.

apple	**117 Calories**
hot dog	**170 Calories**
slice of pizza	**185 Calories**
banana	**100 Calories**
chocolate (oz.)	**155 Calories**
carrot	**25 Calories**
spinach	**23 Calories**

6 Measuring Time

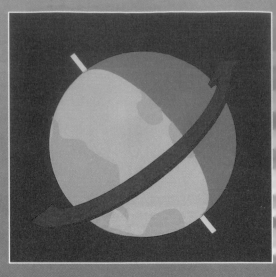

A *day* is the time it takes earth to spin around once on its *axis*, or twenty-four hours. (The axis is an imaginary pole that runs through the middle of the planet from the North Pole to the South Pole.) Seven days make up one *week*. Twenty-eight to thirty-one days make up one *month*. A month is the approximate time needed for the moon to revolve once around earth. The lunar month actually takes twenty-nine days, twelve hours, forty-four minutes, and three seconds.

Twelve months make up one *year*. A year is the time it takes earth to revolve once around the sun, or 365 days, five hours, forty-eight minutes, and forty-six seconds.

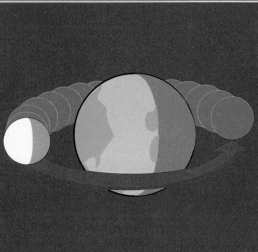

Ancient and Modern Calendars

Calendars are tools that help us group days into weeks, months, and years. The calendar used throughout the world today is called the *Gregorian* calendar. Several other calendars are also in use. Among them are Hebrew, Christian, Eastern Orthodox, Moslem, and Hindu calendars. These calendars start on different days, and divide the year according to different seasons and months.

Most people today use one or two calendars—the Gregorian calendar and a religious calendar. The ancient Egyptians used three calendars at once! One was a calendar divided into 365 days. Another was a farmer's calendar based on the seasons. And the third was a religious calendar.

The Babylonian Calendar

The calendar used in ancient Babylon divided the year into 354 days. The days were grouped into twelve twenty-nine-day "months" or cycles of the moon. Eleven extra days were added at the end of each year to bring this calendar based on moon cycles in line with the 365-day cycle of the sun.

The Egyptian Calendar

The ancient Egyptians used a calendar that divided the year into twelve months of thirty days each. Five days were added at the end of each year to bring the calendar to 365 days.

The Chinese Calendar

The Chinese calendar divides the year into 365 days. It also groups years into cycles of twelve years each. Each year within the cycle is named for an animal.

The Hebrew Calendar

The Hebrew, or Jewish, calendar is a lunar calendar. It is divided into twelve months of twenty-nine to thirty days. An extra month is added to the Hebrew year every nineteen years to bring the calendar in line with the solar year.

ניסן	Nisan	תמוז	Tammuz	תשרי	Tishrei	טבת	Tevet
אייר	Iyar	אב	Av	חשון	Cheshvan	שבט	Shevat
סיון	Sivan	אלול	Elul	כסלו	Kislev	אדר	Adar

Christian Calendars

The calendar of the Christian Church is divided into seasons based on the life of Christ. Over 1,000 years ago, the Church split into eastern and western divisions. Although the holidays celebrated in the eastern and western churches are the same,

> **Advent**
>
> **Christmas**
>
> **Lent**
>
> **Easter**
>
> **Pentecost,**

the calendars are now different from each other so the holidays are celebrated on different days.

The Hindu Calendar

The Hindu calendar is based on lunar "days." There are thirty days in each month. So every Hindu day is 1/30 of the moon's cycle. It is not the same as the solar day.

The Moslem Calendar

The Moslem calendar is a lunar calendar of twelve months of twenty-nine to thirty days each. There is no time added to bring the calendar in line with solar years. Holidays on the Moslem calendar "float" through the seasons as the years pass by.

If Your Birthday is February 29, How Old Are You?

When Sosigenes created the Julian calendar, he divided the year into 365 days. But a solar year is really about 365 1/4 days long.

Sosigenes needed to make up for lost time. He decided to add a twenty-ninth day to February every fourth year. We call these long years *leap years*.

But what if you are born on February 29? Your birthday comes only once every four years. On your first "birthday," are you four years old?

Most leap-year babies celebrate their birthdays on February 28 or March 1 on nonleap years.

The Roman Calendar

The ancient Romans began their year on March 1, the first day of the farming season. The calendar divided the year into ten months and 304 days. The ancient Romans, unlike the Babylonians and Egyptians, didn't add days at the end of the year. After a number of "Roman years," March 1 fell in late summer, and the calendar became useless. It was fixed in 46 B.C. (46 years before the birth of Christ) by the emperor Julius Caesar (see Julian calendar, below).

The Julian Calendar

The astronomer Sosigenes was asked by Julius Caesar to create a calendar for the Roman Empire. The calendar was based on the solar year of 365 days. The year was divided into twelve months. Each month lasted thirty or thirty-one days, with the exception of February, which lasted either twenty-eight or twenty-nine days. The Julian calendar is the basis for the Gregorian calendar. The names used for the months in the Roman calendar were used in the Julian calendar. These names are also used today.

Roman	Gregorian		Roman	Gregorian
Januarius	January		Quintilis	July
Februarius	February		Sextilis	August
Martius	March		September	September
Aprilis	April		October	October
Maius	May		November	November
Junius	June		December	December

Julius Caesar introduced his new calendar in 46 B.C., but he didn't follow his own rules that year. In order to make up for the time lost by the Roman calendar, the emperor added eleven days to the year. In 45 B.C. the year was 365 days long and the seasons matched the calendar.

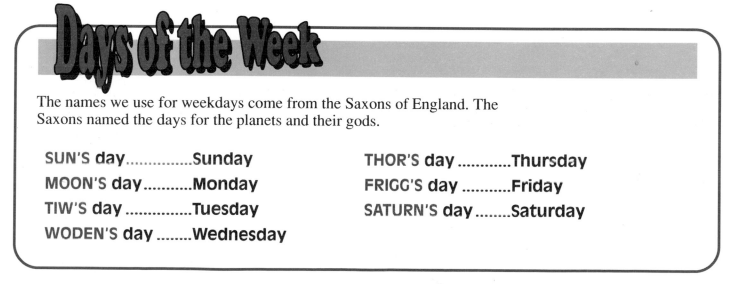

Days of the Week

The names we use for weekdays come from the Saxons of England. The Saxons named the days for the planets and their gods.

SUN'S day.............Sunday   THOR'S day............Thursday

MOON'S day..........Monday   FRIGG'S day...........Friday

TIW'S day..............Tuesday   SATURN'S day........Saturday

WODEN'S day........Wednesday

The Gregorian Calendar

Sosigenes made a mistake in the Julian calendar, but nobody found the mistake for hundreds of years. He made every fourth year a leap year, but these leap years made the calendar too long to measure the cycle of the sun. By the 1500s, the Julian calendar was almost two weeks ahead of the actual solar year.

Pope Gregory VIII fixed the mistake in 1582. Leap years are now added to the calendar every four years except for the years that begin new centuries, unless the number of the new century can be divided evenly by 400.

The century date 1900 was not a leap year (1900 ÷ 400 = 4 3/4), but the year 2000 will be a leap year (2000 ÷ 400 = 5).

Pope Gregory VIII's calendar is accurate to within sixteen seconds per year. That's the reason we still use it today.

JANUARY

SUNDAY	MONDAY	TUESDAY	WEDNESDAY	THURSDAY	FRIDAY	SATURDAY
				1	2	3
4	5	6	7	8	9	10
11	12	13	14	15	16	17
18	19	20	21	22	23	24
25	26	27	28	29	30	31

Ben Franklin and the Lost Days

News of the error in the Julian calendar traveled slowly. It was not until 1752 that the British colonists in North America changed from the Julian to the Gregorian calendar. By that time, the Julian calendar was eleven days off the solar year. To adjust to the new calendar, the colonists simply skipped the days between September 2 and September 14, 1752.

According to Ben Franklin, " . . . those who love their pillow [will] lie down in Peace on the second of this month and not perhaps awake until the morning of the fourteenth."

Clocks

Daylight saving rule: Spring forward, fall back.

We divide **days** into 24 **hour**s, but hours are divided into **60** parts. Why?

The ancient Babylonians used a base 60 method for counting, unlike our base 10, or decimal system (see p. 16). A base 60 system was used to divide the globe into six groups of 60 minutes each, and to divide the hours into 60 equal parts.

Roman astronomers later adopted this system of dividing hours. They called each division a **par minuta** or "small part of an hour." From the Latin name comes our word **minute**. These early astronomers also divided minutes into **60** equal parts. They called each division **par seconda**, or **second**.

Daylight Saving Time

During World War I, clocks in the United States and England were set one hour ahead. By setting the clocks ahead in the summertime, the wartime work day had one more hour of daylight. The clocks were set back in autumn, when daylight hours were shorter anyway. Working in daylight meant saving energy because electric lights weren't needed to light up the factories.

Setting the clocks ahead also meant more hours of daylight for play and leisure activites. When the war ended, people still wanted to enjoy the extra hours of summer daylight. Daylight Saving Time was here to stay!

Not everybody in the United States uses Daylight Saving Time. People in Hawaii and parts of Indiana and Arizona don't reset their clocks. But most Americans set their clocks one hour ahead on the first Sunday in April and back one hour on the last Sunday of October.

MILITARY TIME

Standard Time	24-Hour Time	Military Time	Standard Time	24-Hour Time	Military Time
12:00 midnight	00:00	0000 hours	12:00 noon	12:00	1200 hours
1:00 am	01:00	0100 hours	1:00 pm	13:00	1300 hours
2:00 am	02:00	0200 hours	2:00 pm	14:00	1400 hours
3:00 am	03:00	0300 hours	3:00 pm	15:00	1500 hours
4:00 am	04:00	0400 hours	4:00 pm	16:00	1600 hours
5:00 am	05:00	0500 hours	5:00 pm	17:00	1700 hours
6:00 am	06:00	0600 hours	6:00 pm	18:00	1800 hours
7:00 am	07:00	0700 hours	7:00 pm	19:00	1900 hours
8:00 am	08:00	0800 hours	8:00 pm	20:00	2000 hours
9:00 am	09:00	0900 hours	9:00 pm	21:00	2100 hours
10:00 am	10:00	1000 hours	10:00 pm	22:00	2200 hours
11:00 am	11:00	1100 hours	11:00 pm	23:00	2300 hours
			12:00 midnight	24:00	2400 hours

Standard time can be confusing. For example, eight o'clock can mean eight in the morning or eight in the evening. To avoid confusion, scientists created a 24-hour clock. The hours are numbered **1** through **24**, beginning at midnight. This way of counting the hours in a day is called **military time**. People who use military time say the time in a special way. For example, 11:00 is not called "eleven o'clock," but "eleven hundred hours."

Beyond Standard Time

Standard time means the measurement of the day in two blocks of twelve hours each. The twelve hours from midnight to noon are *a.m.* hours. The twelve hours from noon until midnight are *p.m.* hours. The abbreviations "a.m." and "p.m." come from the Latin for *ante meridiem* and *post meridiem*, meaning *before* (ante) and *after* (post) midday or noon *(meridiem)*.

Shadow Sticks

Among the earliest timepieces were *shadow sticks.* The length and direction of the stick's shadow changes as the sun moves across the sky. The length and direction of a shadow give a rough idea of the time of day.

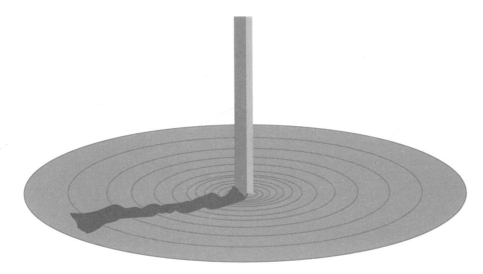

Sundials

Like *shadow sticks, sundials* use shadows to show the time. Sundials, however, have a face with numbers that stand for the hours of sunlight. A stick, or *gnomon,* casts a shadow that falls on the face. The time is told by reading the number on the face where the shadow falls. But you can only tell time on a sunny day!

Water Clocks

Water clocks are made by *calibrating,* or marking, the inside of a container that has a hole in its bottom. The container is filled with water and the water drips out slowly through the hole. Time is told by reading the water level in the container.

Over 3,000 years ago, the ancient Egyptians used water clocks called *clepsydras*. The Greeks and Romans used more complicated water clocks. Water was dripped from a reservoir, or a "holding tank," into a watertight cylinder. Time was told by reading a float in the cylinder.

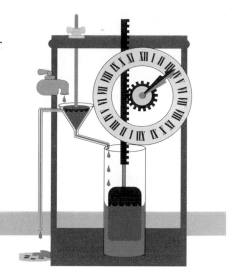

Lamps and Candle Clocks

The level of oil in a lamp shows how long the lamp has been burning. Reading the level of oil in a lit lamp or even the changes in length of a burning candle were other methods for telling time.

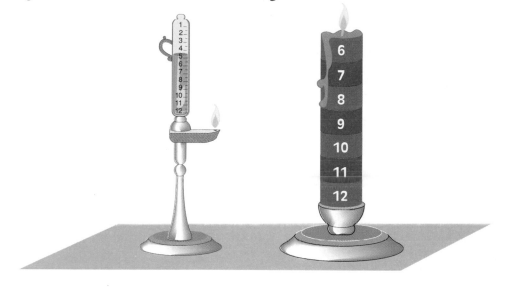

Sandglasses

Sandglasses were invented hundreds of years ago. They are still used today as kitchen timers. Sandglasses have two chambers connected by a narrow neck. One chamber is filled with sand. When the sandglass is turned upside down or inverted, sand drips through the neck from the upper to the lower chamber. Time is measured when all the sand has passed to the lower chamber. In large sandglasses, or hourglasses, it takes sixty minutes for the sand to pass from the upper chamber to the lower chamber.

Mechanical Clocks

Mechanical clocks were invented over 700 years ago. The first mechanical clocks didn't have hands and faces. Instead, they told the time with bells or chimes that rang out on the hours.

Italian astronomer and inventor Galileo Galilei (1564-1642) discovered that a swinging pendulum could keep time evenly. But it wasn't until 1657 that the first pendulum clock was invented. It was made by Dutch mathematician Christiaan Huygens (1629-1695).

Huygens's clock used swinging pendulums controlled by gears. The gears moved the hands of the clock across the clock face. Later, scientists discovered that a pendulum one meter long takes one second to complete a full arc backwards and forwards. Around 1670, the first grandfather clocks were built with pendulums one meter long.

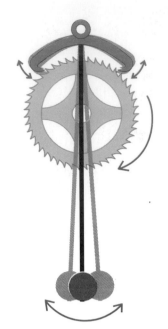

Quartz

Today many clocks and watches use the battery-powered vibrations of a quartz crystal to keep time. The natural vibration of a quartz crystal is 100,000 times per second. Modern clocks and watches show the time in digital as well as analog displays.

Digital   Analog

Atomic hydrogen masers, or "atomic clocks," are the most accurate clocks. They are accurate to within one second in 1.7 million years. Hydrogen atoms make atomic clocks work. A hydrogen atom vibrates 9.2 billion times in one second.

Seconds, Please!

Seconds really add up. Have you ever wondered how many seconds there are in:

One Minute	=	60 seconds	**Five Years**	=	1,103,760,00 seconds
One Hour	=	3,600 seconds	**Ten Years**	=	2,207,520,00 seconds
One Day	=	86,400 seconds	**Fifty Years**	=	11,037,600,000 seconds
One Week	=	604,800 seconds	**One Hundred Years**	=	22,075,200,000 seconds
One Year	=	220,752,000 seconds			

Greenwich Mean Time

The sun reaches its highest point in the sky at different times in different places around the world. That's why the earth is divided into twenty-four time zones, one zone for each hour of the day. These time zones loosely follow lines of longitude.

    The time zones begin at the *prime meridian* in Greenwich, England, and meet at the *International Date Line*. If you travel east over the International Date Line, you start the day over again. If you travel west over the line, you jump ahead to the next day.

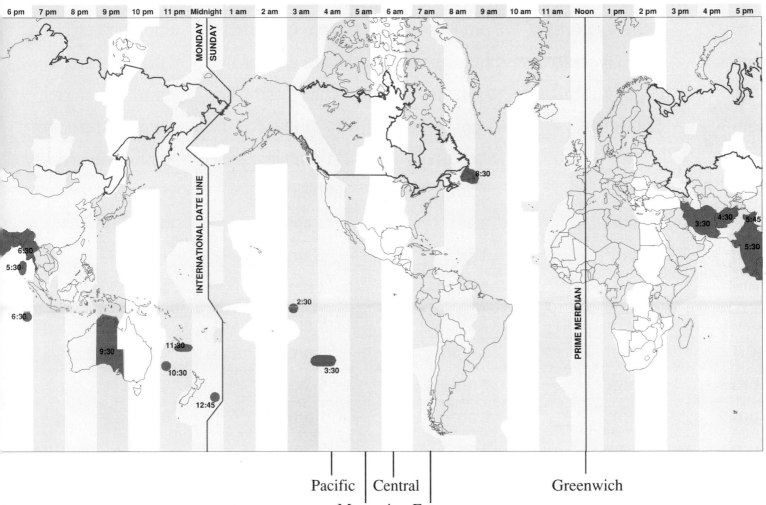

Table of Greenwich Mean and U.S. Standard Time Equivalents

Greenwich	Eastern Time	Central Time	Mountain Time	Pacific Time
MIDNIGHT	7 pm (yesterday)	6 pm (yesterday)	5 pm (yesterday)	4 pm (yesterday)
1 am	8 pm (yesterday)	7 pm (yesterday)	6 pm (yesterday)	5 pm (yesterday)
2 am	9 pm (yesterday)	8 pm (yesterday)	7 pm (yesterday)	6 pm (yesterday)
3 am	10 pm (yesterday)	9 pm (yesterday)	8 pm (yesterday)	7 pm (yesterday)
4 am	11 pm (yesterday)	10 pm (yesterday)	9 pm (yesterday)	8 pm (yesterday)
5 am	MIDNIGHT	11 pm (yesterday)	10 pm (yesterday)	9 pm (yesterday)
6 am	1 am	MIDNIGHT	11 pm (yesterday)	10 pm (yesterday)
7 am	2 am	1 am	MIDNIGHT	11 pm (yesterday)
8 am	3 am	2 am	1 am	MIDNIGHT
9 am	4 am	3 am	2 am	1 am
10 am	5 am	4 am	3 am	2 am
11 am	6 am	5 am	4 am	3 am
NOON	7 am	6 am	5 am	4 am
1 pm	8 am	7 am	6 am	5 am
2 pm	9 am	8 am	7 am	6 am
3 pm	10 am	9 am	8 am	7 am
4 pm	11 am	10 am	9 am	8 am
5 pm	NOON	11 am	10 am	9 am
6 pm	1 pm	NOON	11 am	10 am
7 pm	2 pm	1 pm	NOON	11 am
8 pm	3 pm	2 pm	1 pm	NOON
9 pm	4 pm	3 pm	2 pm	1 pm
10 pm	5 pm	4 pm	3 pm	2 pm
11 pm	6 pm	5 pm	4 pm	3 pm

GEOMETRY

1 Geometric Shapes

Geometry is the branch of mathematics that explains how **points**, **lines**, **planes**, and **shapes** are related.

Points

Points have no size or dimensions, that is, no width, length, or height. They are an **idea** and cannot be seen. But, points are used to tell the position of lines and objects. Points are usually named with capital letters:

A, B, C, D and so on.

Points can describe where things begin or end.

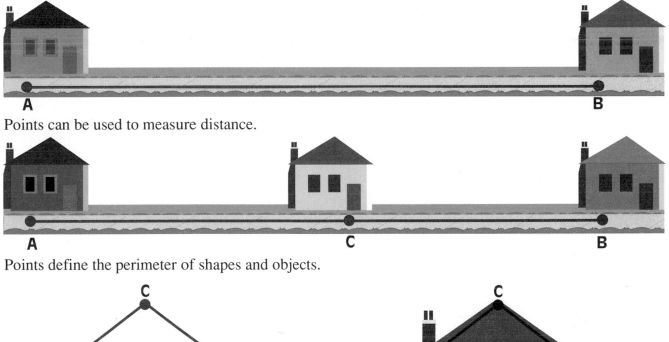

A   B

Points can be used to measure distance.

A   C   B

Points define the perimeter of shapes and objects.

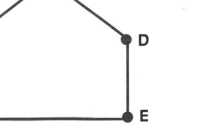

Lines

Lines extend without ending in opposite directions. Like points, lines have no dimension, but they have infinite length. Lines are named by points with a line symbol written above.

$\overleftrightarrow{AB}$

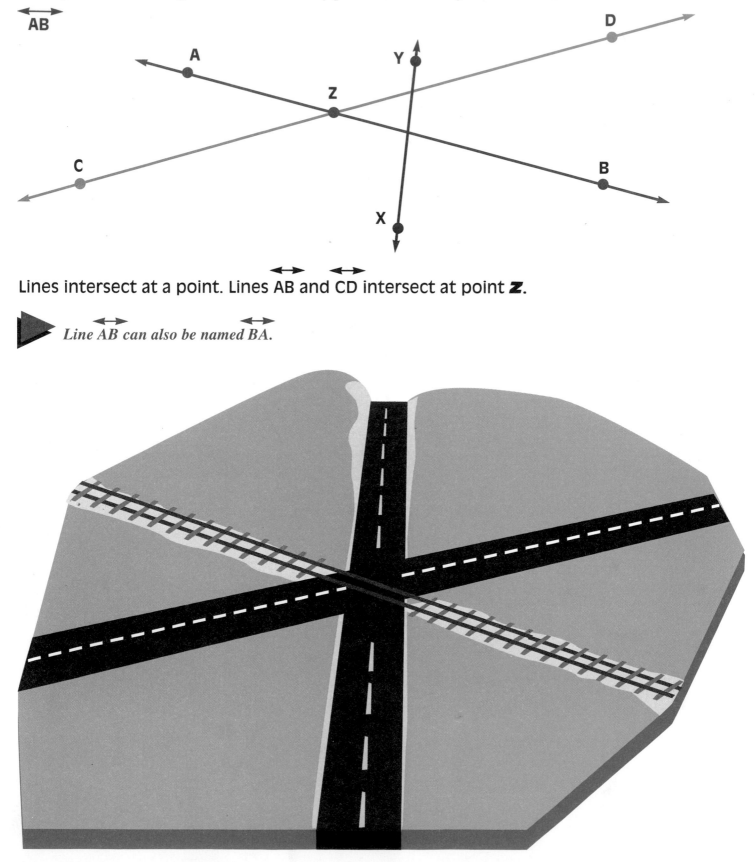

Lines intersect at a point. Lines $\overleftrightarrow{AB}$ and $\overleftrightarrow{CD}$ intersect at point **Z**.

▶ *Line $\overleftrightarrow{AB}$ can also be named $\overleftrightarrow{BA}$.*

Line Segments

Line segments are parts of lines defined by two endpoints along the line. They have *length*.

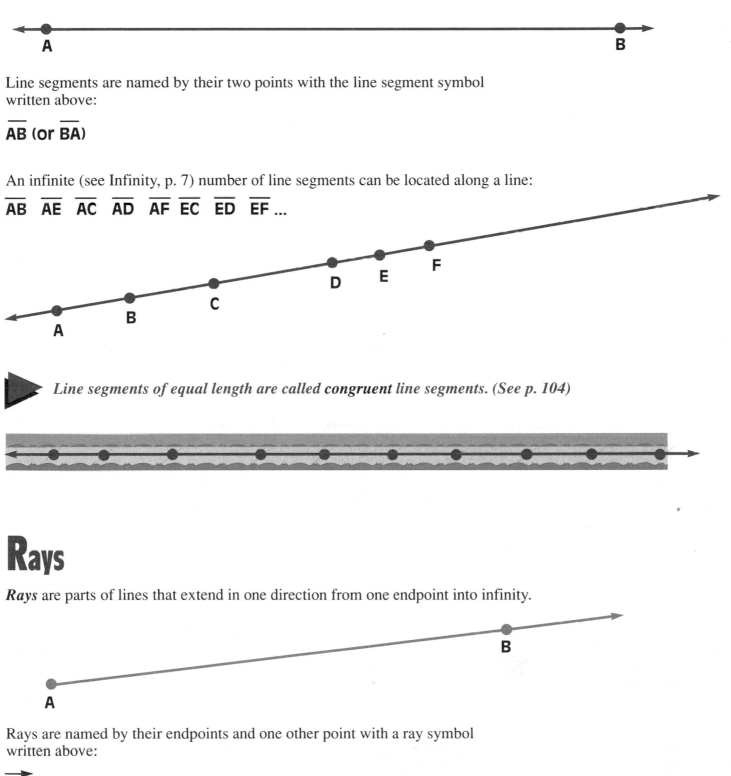

Line segments are named by their two points with the line segment symbol written above:

$\overline{AB}$ (or $\overline{BA}$)

An infinite (see Infinity, p. 7) number of line segments can be located along a line:
$\overline{AB}$ $\overline{AE}$ $\overline{AC}$ $\overline{AD}$ $\overline{AF}$ $\overline{EC}$ $\overline{ED}$ $\overline{EF}$ ...

▶ *Line segments of equal length are called* **congruent** *line segments.* (See p. 104)

Rays

Rays are parts of lines that extend in one direction from one endpoint into infinity.

Rays are named by their endpoints and one other point with a ray symbol written above:

$\overrightarrow{AB}$

Parallel Lines

Parallel lines are lines within the same plane. Because they are always the same distance apart, parallel lines continue to infinity without intersecting or touching at any point.

The symbol for parallel lines is // and is read "is parallel to."

AB // CD

Intersecting Lines

Intersecting lines are lines in the same plane. Intersecting lines meet and pass through one another at one point.

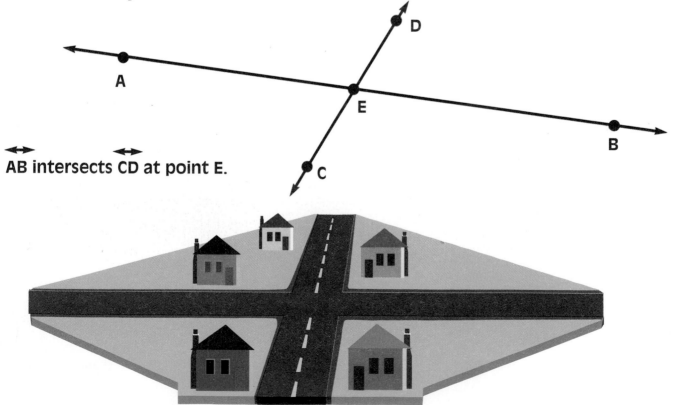

AB intersects CD at point E.

Perpendicular Lines

Perpendicular lines are intersecting lines that form right angles.

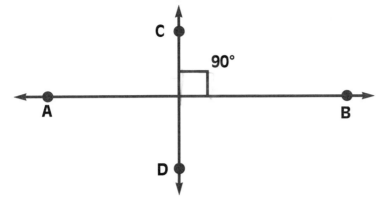

The symbol for perpendicular lines is ⊥ and is read "is perpendicular to."

AB ⊥ CD

Planes

Planes are an infinite set of points on a flat surface. Planes extend in all directions to infinity.

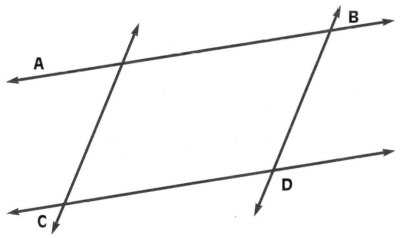

Planes are named with capital letters written after the word "Plane."

Plane ABCD

95

Angles

Angles are formed by two rays with a common endpoint called a *vertex*.

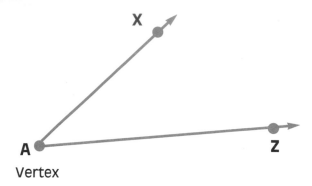

Vertex

Angles are named by writing the names of three points on the set of lines after the symbol for angle, or by naming only the middle point after the angle symbol. The middle point always names the vertex.

$\angle$ **XAZ** or $\angle$ **ZAX** or $\angle$ **A**

Angles come in different shapes and sizes. Some are narrow, some are wide. But all angles can be measured as part of a circle. To make calculations easy, scientists have developed the protractor, a kind of ruler for angles.

Angles are measured in degrees from 0° to 180°.

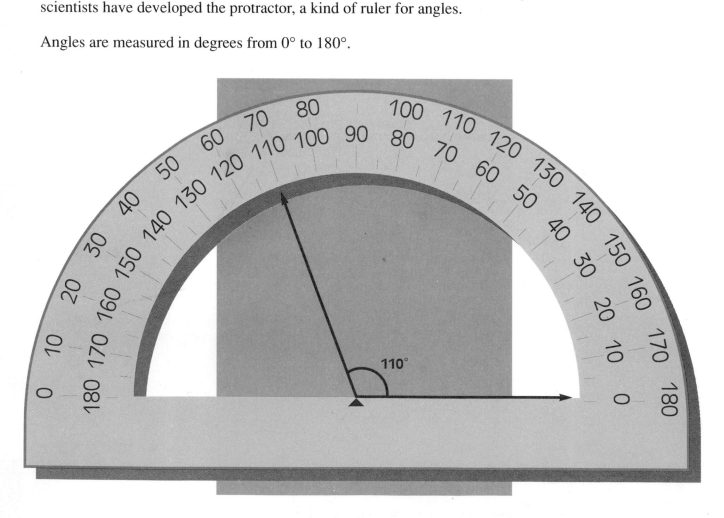

Acute Angles

Acute angles are angles that measure less than 90°.

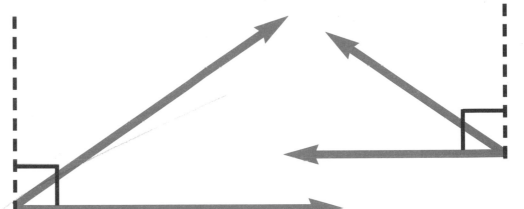

Obtuse Angles

Obtuse angles are angles that measure more than 90° and less than 180°.

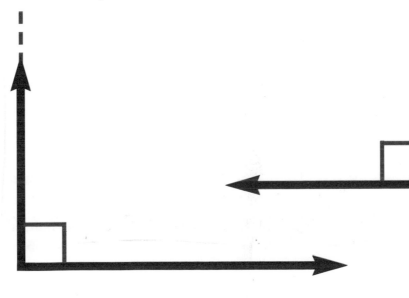

Right Angles

Right angles are angles that measure exactly 90°.

Reflex Angles

Reflex angles are angles that measure more than 180°, but less than 360°.

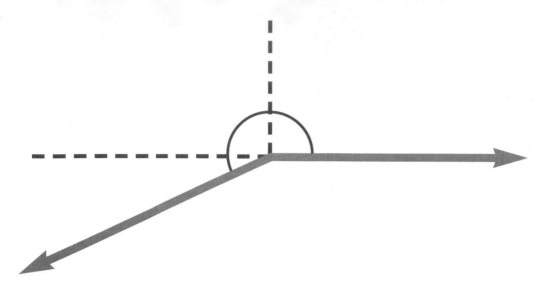

Complementary Angles

Complementary angles are angles that, when joined together, form a right angle (90°).

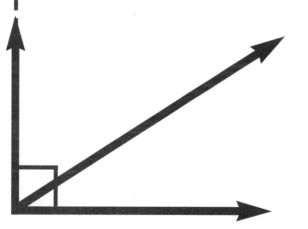

Supplementary Angles

Supplementary angles are angles that, when joined together, form a straight line (180°).

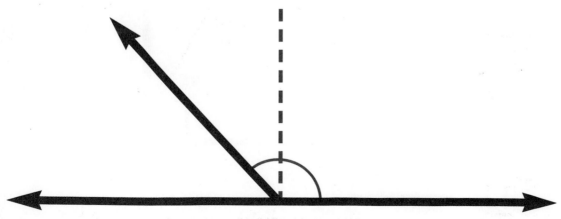

Polygons

Polygons are two-dimensional. or flat shapes, formed from three or more line segments that lie within one plane. The line segments form angles that meet at points called *vertexes*. Polygons come in many shapes and sizes, including:

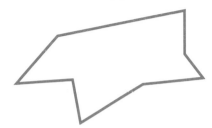

concave polygons

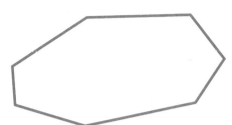

convex polygons

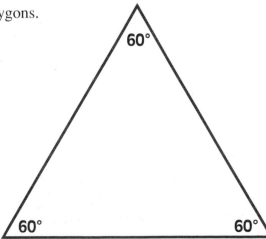

 Polygons are usually irregular or regular. Irregular polygons are made up of unequal sides and unequal angles. Regular polygons have sides of equal length and angles of equal size.

Squares and equilateral triangles are examples of regular polygons.

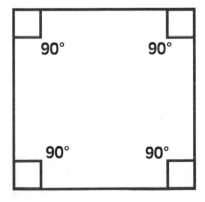

Triangles

Triangles are polygons that have three sides and three vertexes.

Right triangles are formed when two of three line segments meet in 90 degree angles. In a right triangle, the longest side has a special name: the *hypotenuse.*

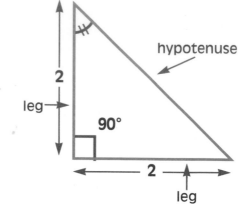

Isosceles triangles have two sides of equal length.

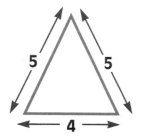

Scalene triangles have no sides of equal length.

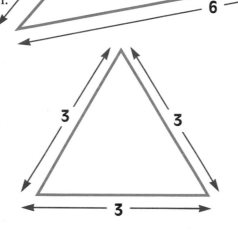

Equilateral triangles have three sides of equal length.

Pythagoras's Great Idea

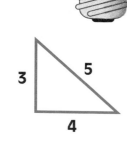

Pythagoras (ca.582–ca.497 B.C.) was a Greek philosopher and mathematician. His ideas influenced great thinkers throughout the ages, and he is well known to math students. His Pythagorian Theorem is a simple rule about the proportion of the sides of right triangles: *The square of the hypotenuse of a right triangle is equal to the sum of the square of the other two sides.*

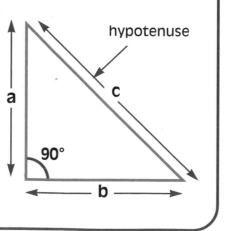

$$a^2 + b^2 = c^2$$
$$3^2 \div 4^2 = 5^2 \quad 9 + 16 = 25 \quad 25 = 25$$

Quadrilaterals

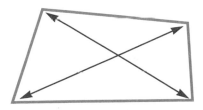

Quadrilaterals are polygons that have four sides and four vertices.

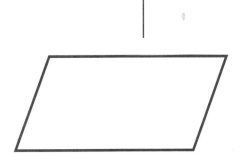

Parallelograms are quadrilaterals that have parallel line segments in both pairs of opposite sides.

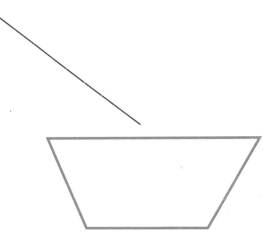

Trapezoids are quadrilaterals that have parallel sides.

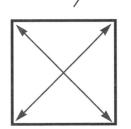

Squares are rectangles that have sides of equal length.

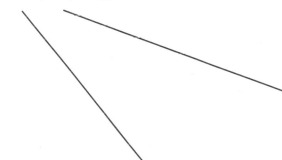

Rectangles are parallelograms formed by line segments that meet at right angles. A rectangle always has four right angles.

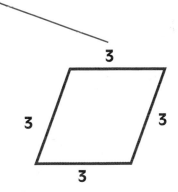

Rhombuses are parallelograms that have sides of equal length.

Other Common Polygons

Pentagons

Pentagons are polygons that have five sides and five vertices.

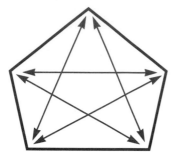

Hexagons

Hexagons are polygons that have six sides and six vertices.

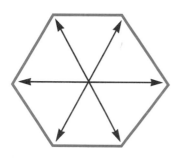

Octagons

Octagons are polygons that have eight sides and eight vertices.

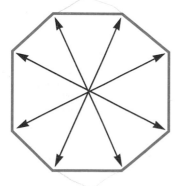

Polygons

Name	Number of sides
triangle	3
quadrilateral	4
square	4 equal and perpendicular
rectangle	4 perpendicular
rhombus	4 equal opposite parallel
parallelogram	4 opposite parallel
pentagon	5
hexagon	6
heptagon	7
octagon	8
nonagon	9
decagon	10
ondecagon or hendecagon	11
dodecagon	12
icosagon	20

Circles

A *circle* is a set of points within a plane. Each point on the circle is at an equal distance from a common point inside the circle called the *center*.

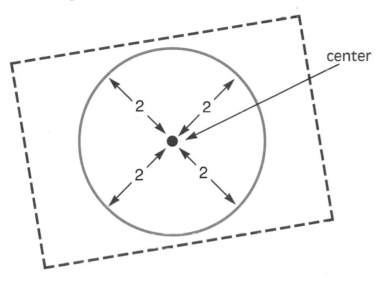

center

The distance from the center of the circle to any point on the circle is called the *radius*.

r = radius

A line segment drawn through the center of the circle to points on either side of the circle is called the *diameter*. The circle is bisected or cut into two equal parts along the diameter line. Diameter is equal to two times the radius.

2r = diameter

The distance around the circle is called the *circumference* (see p. 72).

$$\left. \begin{matrix} \pi d \\ \text{or} \\ 2\pi r \end{matrix} \right\} = \text{circumference}$$

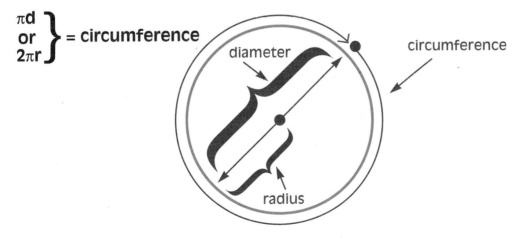

diameter

circumference

radius

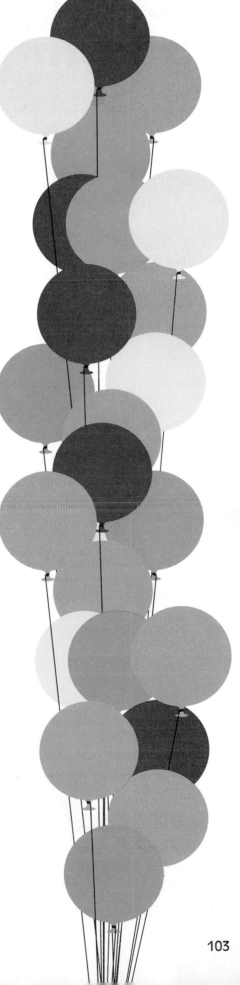

2 Symmetry, Congruence, and Similarity

Symmetry surrounds us. It is found in art and architecture, music, plants, insects, animals—and humans.

Symmetry is the exact matching of shapes or figures on opposite sides of dividing lines or around a central point. The dividing line is called the **axis of symmetry** or **line of symmetry**. Certain shapes, particularly polygons and circles, have many lines of symmetry.

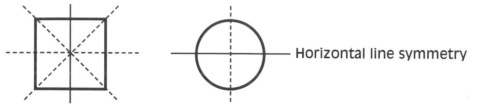

Horizontal line symmetry

Vertical line symmetry

Congruence refers to two shapes of exactly the same size and shape.

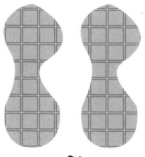

▶ *The symbol for congruence is* ≅ *and is read "is congruent to."*

The Elements of Geometry

Euclid (lived ca. 300 B.C.), a Greek mathematician who lived in Alexandria, Egypt, wrote one of the most famous textbooks of all time, **The Elements of Geometry**. Many people believe that Euclid's book has been read by more people than any other book except the Bible. Even our modern books on geometry are based on Euclid's 2,000-year-old teachings.

The symmetrical shapes formed by drawing lines of symmetry often create congruent shapes. But symmetrical figures are not necessarily congruent.

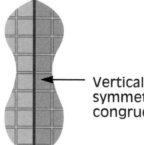

Vertical line of symmetry makes congruent shapes

Horizontal line does not

Similarity means objects have the same shape but they are not necessarily identical in size.

So congruent shapes are always similar.

3 Objects in Three Dimensions

Polygons and circles are flat, or two-dimensional. They have only length and width. But *cubes, prisms, pyramids,* and *spheres* are solid. They have a third dimension known as height or, sometimes, depth. These solids are also called *space figures*.

Cubes, prisms, pyramids, and other solids have sides called *faces*. These faces are flat surfaces that are in the shapes of polygons. Faces meet at edges. The edges are line segments, which meet in vertexes. The vertexes are points (see p. 91).

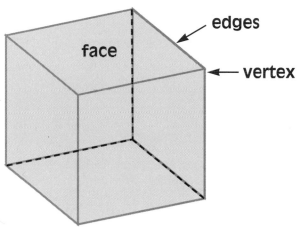

Cubes

Cubes have six faces. Each face is a square.

Prisms

Prisms have two parallel, congruent polygon-shaped *bases.* The sides of prisms are all parallelograms. Prisms can have an infinite variety of shapes because of the endless number of polygon shapes that can be used as bases. Each face that is not a base is called a *lateral face.*

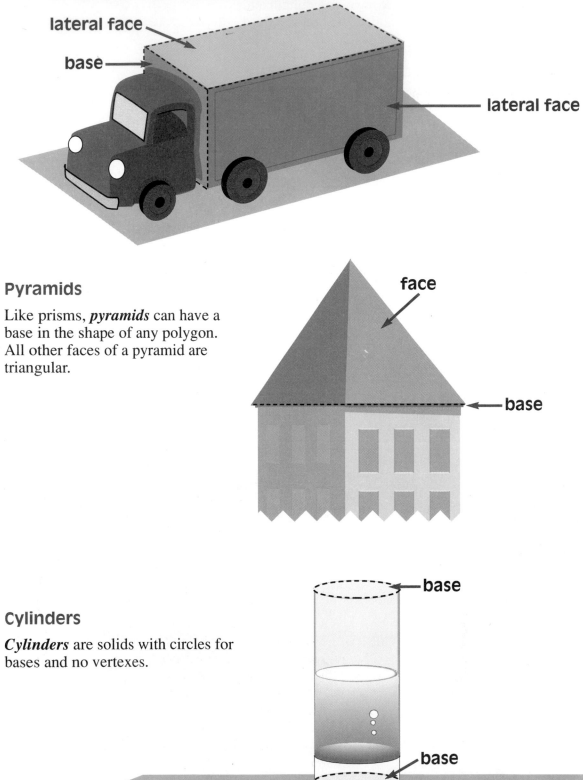

Pyramids

Like prisms, *pyramids* can have a base in the shape of any polygon. All other faces of a pyramid are triangular.

Cylinders

Cylinders are solids with circles for bases and no vertexes.

Cones

Cones have one flat, circular base and rise to a point. They have one base and one vertex.

vertex

base

Spheres

Spheres have no flat faces and no vertexes. A sphere has an outline of a circle when viewed from any angle.

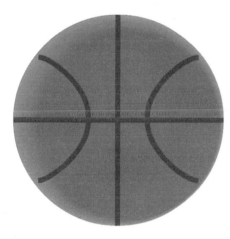

FEWER FACETS

You can draw regular polygons (polygons with equal sides and angles) with any number of sides. However, you can't form an infinite number of regular solids (solids with equal sides and angles). In fact, you can form only five: *tetrahedron, cube, octahedron, dodecahedron,* and *icosahedron.*

MONEY AND MONETARY SYSTEMS

1 U.S. Currency

Mint Condition

dollar

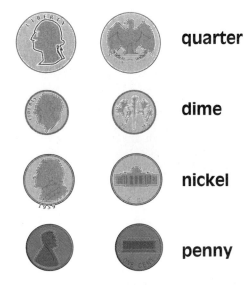

quarter

dime

nickel

penny

British currency is made up of **pounds** and **pence.** The Germans use **Marks** and **Pfennigs.** Why do we use dollars and cents?

The word **dollar** comes from the German word for a large silver coin, the **Thaler.** In 1781, **cent** was suggested as a name for the smallest division of the dollar. Thomas Jefferson, third President of the United States and an amateur scientist, thought that the dollar should be divided into 100 parts. The word **cent** comes from the Latin **centum**, which means one hundred.

There is a smaller value of U.S. money than the cent, although there is no coin for it. The value is called the **mill.** It is worth 1/10th of a cent, or $.001.

Place Value and American Money

American money is created in decimal-based currency. That means we can add, subtract, divide, and multiply money the same way we do any decimal numbers (see p. 46).

The basic unit of U.S. currency is the dollar. The dollar has the value of one on a place value chart. The decimal point separates dollars from cents, which are counted as tenths and hundredths in a place value chart.

$1.11	hundreds = dollars	.	ten = dimes	one = pennies
one cent				1
ten cents		.	1	0
one dollar	1	.	0	0

$4.63	hundreds = dollars	.	ten = dimes	one = pennies
three cents				3
sixty cents		.	6	0
four dollars	4	.	0	0

What's money? What's currency?

Money is anything you can trade for something else. If you trade a sandwich for a can of root beer, you're using the sandwich as money.

Currency is the set of coins and bills issued by a government to be used as money. Not all money is currency. Before coins and bills became currency, humans used a variety of items as money. Stone disks, fur pelts, beads, and feathers have all served the purpose. And when coins were created, they were valued against the old items commonly traded as money. In ancient Greece, for example, the silver coin called the **drachma** was equal to a handful of iron nails. Since a handful of iron nails was the price for an ox, one **drachma** could buy one ox.

When you write down amounts of money using the dollar sign, $, you write the amounts the same way as you write decimal numbers—in decimal notation. There is a separate cents sign, ¢. The cents sign does not use decimal notation. So if you have to add cents to dollars, you have to change cents to dollar notation.

$$8¢ = \$ .08$$
$$36¢ = \$ .36$$

To add 8¢ to $1.03, convert the 8¢ notation to its decimal form, $.08. Then add the decimal fractions.

$$
\begin{array}{r}
8¢ = \$ \ .08 \\
+ \ \$1.03 \\
\hline
\$1.11
\end{array}
$$

Cents in Dollar Notation

¢	to	$
1		.01
2		.02
3		.03
4		.04
5		.05
10		.10
25		.25
100		1.00

Money Talks

break the bank	spend more than you have
broke	out of money
bucks	slang for "dollar bills"
budget	a plan for spending money over a period of time
cash	money in coins and bills
C-note	slang for "hundred-dollar bill"
dough	slang for "money"
(a) grand	slang for "thousand dollars"
greenbacks	U.S. paper money
moolah	slang for "money"
sawbuck	slang for "ten-dollar bill"
two bits	slang for "25¢"

2 Other Currency Systems

Money in Other Countries

Countries	Name	Foreign currency in dollars (changes daily)
Argentina	Peso	1.01
Belgium	Franc	.02
Britain	Pound	1.5
China	Yuan	.17
Denmark	Krone	.15
France	Franc	.17
Germany	Mark	.58
India	Rupee	.03
Ireland	Punt	1.43
Israel	Shekel	.34
Italy	Lira	.0005
Japan	Yen	.008
Mexico	Peso	.32
The Netherlands	Guilder	.52
Saudi Arabia	Riyal	.26
Thailand	Bhat	.03

Using this chart, to change a U.S. dollar to British pounds, you divide $1 ÷ 1.5 = £.66 British. To change a British pound to U.S. dollars, you multiply £1 x 1.5 = $1.50 U.S.

GRAPHS

1 Plotting Information

A *graph* is a kind of drawing or diagram that shows *data*, or information, usually in numbers. In order to make a graph, you must first have data.

Making a Grid

Many graphs show information on a *grid*. The grid is made up of lines that intersect to create a screen pattern. The bottom line of the grid is called the *horizontal axis* and the vertical line on the left or right is called the *vertical axis*.

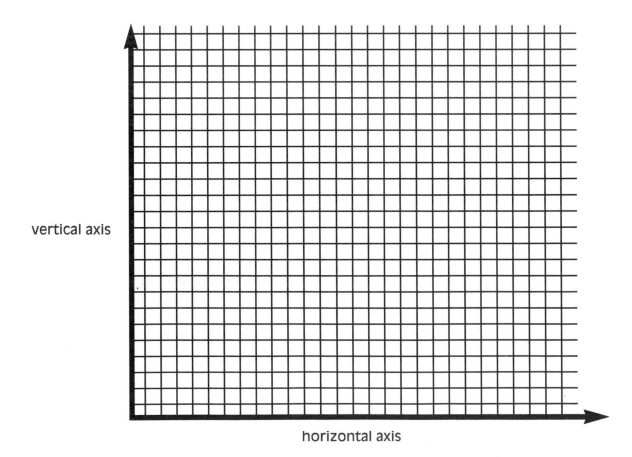

vertical axis

horizontal axis

Plotting and Locating Information on a Grid

To plot or locate points on a grid, first locate the point according to its distance from *0* on the horizontal axis. Then move vertically the appropriate number of units to the next point.

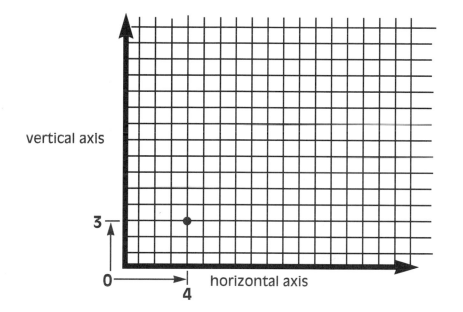

A point on a grid is located by using an ordered pair. An ordered pair lists the horizontal and then the vertical location of the point. Ordered pairs are always written inside parentheses ( ). The ordered pair describing the point J below is (4, 3).

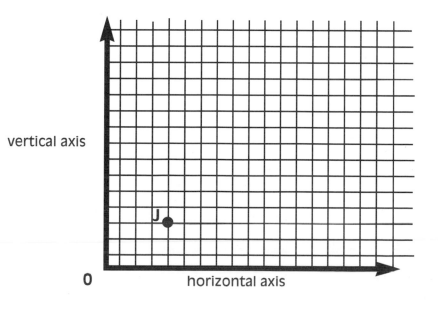

Points located on the same grid are called **coordinate points or coordinates**.

2 Four Kinds of Graphs

Bar Graphs

Bar graphs are used to compare data. They can be *simple* or *complex.*
A simple bar graph can be made complex by adding data.

The Student Council at Jefferson Elementary held an ice cream eating contest at the school fair.

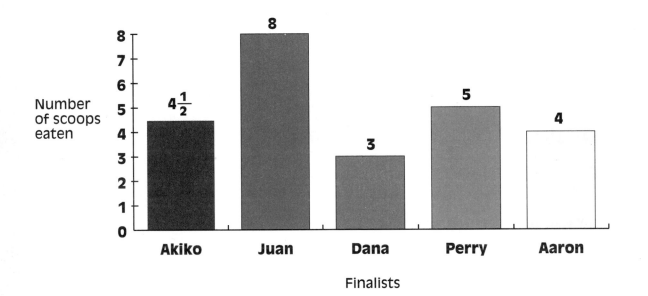

To raise money for the Student Council, student teams sold tickets to the fair.

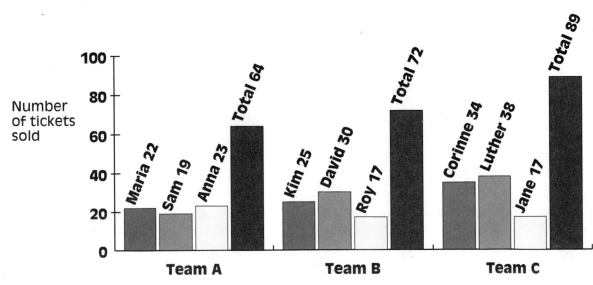

Pictographs

Pictographs are graphs that use pictures called *icons* to display data. Pictographs are used to show data in a small space. Pictographs, like bar graphs, compare data. Because pictographs use icons, however, they also include keys, or definitions of the icons.

Number of tickets sold   = 10 tickets

Number of ice cream scoops eaten

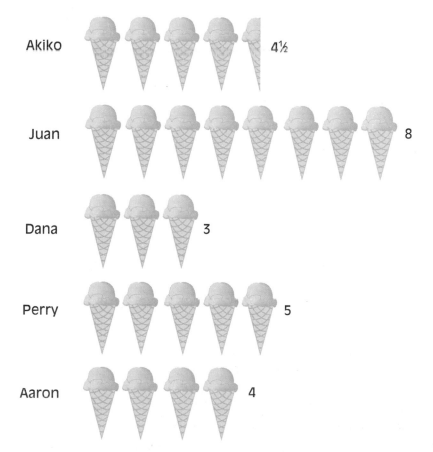

Line Graphs

Line graphs, unlike bar graphs and pictographs, show gradual changes in data.

The Student Council sold tickets to the school fair over a period of three weeks.

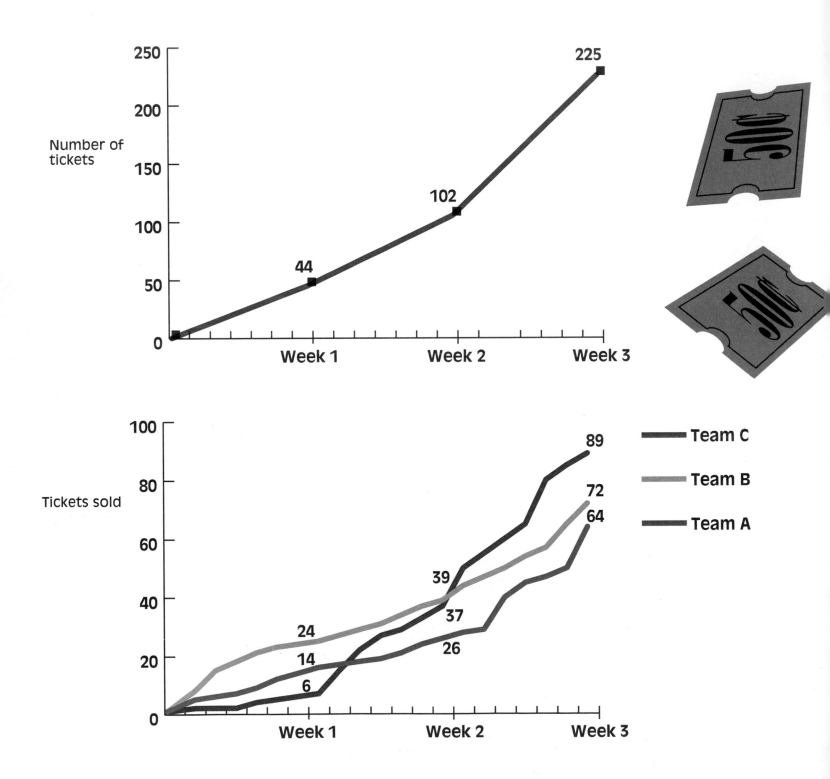

Circle Graphs

Circle graphs are also known as "pie" graphs, or pie charts. Circle graphs consist of a circle divided into parts. The different parts show the different proportions, or amounts, sizes, or numbers of various data.

Number of ice cream scoops eaten in the contest

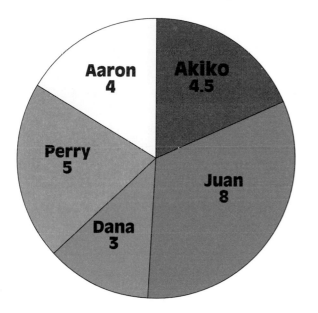

Team ticket sales for school fair, by team

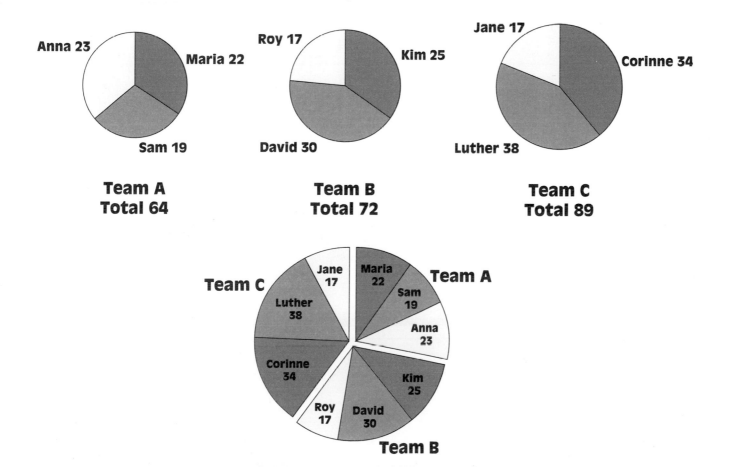

Team A
Total 64

Team B
Total 72

Team C
Total 89

STATISTICS AND PROBABILITY

1 What Is Statistics?

Statistics is a branch of mathematics in which groups of numbers are compared. Statistics includes collecting, organizing, and interpreting data. Your attendance record at school provides your teachers with statistics on your participation in the classroom. Senators' voting attendance records on Capitol Hill are statistics that help us decide if they're doing a good job. Statistics are also used to compare athletes' achievements.

	Minutes	Free Throws	Fouls	Points
Anita	25	6	3	12
Jane	14	4	3	8
Caitlin	22	7	4	16
Josie	19	5	2	14
Tanisha	30	6	5	21
			Total	71

Statistics are often compared in graphs (see Graphs, pp. 112–117).

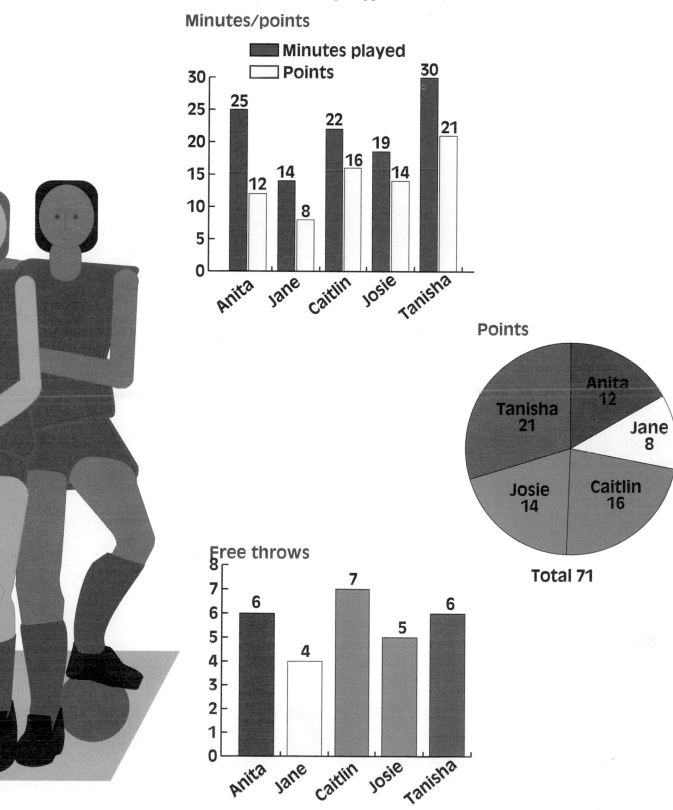

Minutes/points

- ■ Minutes played
- □ Points

	Anita	Jane	Caitlin	Josie	Tanisha
Minutes played	25	14	22	19	30
Points	12	8	16	14	21

Points

- Tanisha 21
- Anita 12
- Jane 8
- Caitlin 16
- Josie 14

Total 71

Free throws

	Anita	Jane	Caitlin	Josie	Tanisha
Free throws	6	4	7	5	6

The Language of Statistics

Range, *median*, *mode*, and *mean* are the basic tools of statistics.

Range

Range is the difference between the greatest and least number in a set of data.

	Minutes	Free Throws	Fouls	Points
Anita	25	6	3	12
Jane	14	4	3	8
Caitlin	22	7	4	16
Josie	19	5	2	14
Tanisha	30	6	5	21
Range	16	3	3	13

 In an even-numbered set of data, the median is usually expressed as both middle numbers. Sometimes the median is expressed as the average of the two middle numbers.

Median

Median is the middle number in a set of data. To find the median, arrange the numbers in order from least to greatest. The number in the middle is the **median.**

	Minutes
Tanisha	30
Anita	25
Caitlin	22
Josie	19
Jane	14

Mode

Mode is the number that appears most often in a set of data. Some sets of data have no mode. Other sets have two or more modes.

	Minutes	Free Throws	Fouls	Points
Anita	25	6	3	12
Jane	14	4	3	8
Caitlin	22	7	4	16
Josie	19	5	2	14
Tanisha	30	6	5	21
Mode		6	3	

Mean

Mean is the average number in a set of data (see Averages, p. 52).

	Minutes	Free Throws	Fouls	Points
Anita	25	6	3	12
Jane	14	4	3	8
Caitlin	22	7	4	16
Josie	19	5	2	14
Tanisha	30	6	5	21
Mean	22	5.6	3.4	14.2

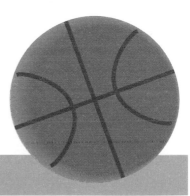

2 Probability

What Is Probability?

Probability means the chance or likelihood that something will happen. In math, probability is a number that is used to describe that chance. The number is always between zero and one. *Zero* means *zero chance* that something will happen. *One* means that *something is certain to happen*. The closer the probability is to *1*, the greater the chance that something will happen.

If you toss a coin, one of two things will result: heads or tails. Both a result of heads and a result of tails are possible, so the probability is *greater than zero*. But a result of heads is not certain, so the probability is *less than one*. In fact, the probability that heads will come up is *one chance in two*, or 1/2.

The Language of Probability

Probability is expressed in one of two ways: in *ratios* or *percentages* (see Ratios and Percentages, pages 48–49).

1:2 or 50%
one in two chance of tossing heads

1:3 or 33.3%
one in three chance of drawing the red ball

1:6 or 16.7%
one in six chance of rolling the five

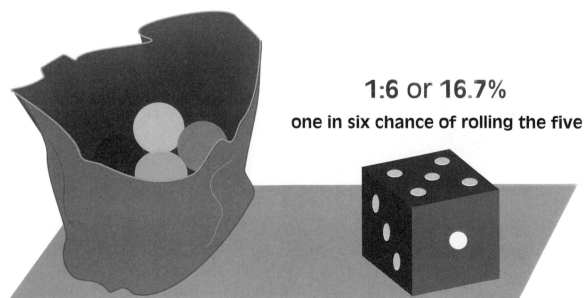

The Gambler's Dilemma: Probability and Statistics in Action

If you toss a coin, the probability of it coming up heads is *1:2*. In gambler's terms, heads is a *50/50* bet. (The term *50/50* means *50%* probability.) You have as much chance of winning with heads as you do on tails in the single toss of the coin.

Big Loser

Say you've bet heads on fifty coin tosses, but each time the coin has come up tails. What is the probability that heads will come up on the fifty-first toss? The probability doesn't change, no matter how many times you toss the coin. Each coin toss has a 1:2 probability of coming up heads.

Why the Dilemma?

Many people believe their chances of tossing heads improves after a long string of tossing tails. In fact, the chance of the coin landing heads up is no greater than it was on the first toss, 1:2, or 50%. But this belief illustrates the difference between probability and statistics.

Statistics are sometimes confused with probability, creating the gambler's dilemma. Toss a coin fifty times. Write down each result by noting the number of times heads came up in the fifty tosses. Then examine your data. Compare the number of times you got heads to the median number for fifty— twenty-five. Then compare your results to the mean number for fifty—also twenty-five. Both the mean and median numbers suggest that heads should come up twenty-five times.

Back to the unhappy gambler. Fifty coin tosses have not produced a heads result. Statistics suggest that heads should have come up twenty-five times. But probability for heads in any one toss of the coin remains *1 in 2*.

Remember, statistics and probability are different things. You can bet on it!

COMPUTERS AND CALCULATORS

1 The Abacus

Long before calculators and computers, people counted on the *abacus*. The abacus is a simple arithmetic machine built during the Chinese Sung dynasty. The abacus greatly increased the speed with which mathematicians could solve arithmetic problems.

The abacus soon became popular throughout the world. Students, as well as scientists and mathematicians, learned to calculate on this marvelous machine.

The abacus consists of nine rows of beads strung on a framework of parallel wires. The beads are separated by a crossbar, forming two sections called "heaven" and "earth." There are two beads in each column of heaven. Each bead in heaven has a value of five. There are five beads in each column of earth. Each bead in earth has a value of *1*. Each column of beads has a value that increases by a power of *10*—just like our decimal system.

2 Simple Calculators

Early Calculators

Blaise Pascal (1623-1662) was a French mathematician and scientist. In 1642, at age 19, he invented the first calculator for adding and subtracting. Unlike the abacus, Pascal's calculator was very expensive and difficult to make. It never caught on. Then in 1671, Gottfried Wilhelm Leibniz invented a calculator that could multiply and divide numbers. Leibniz's machine was also expensive and complicated. Like Pascal's calculator, it never caught on.

Charles Babbage (1792-1871) began work in 1823 on a calculating machine that would solve arithmetic problems and then print out the answers. The machine was run with gear wheels. It was slow. It was so complicated that Babbage died before he finished building it.

Modern Calculators

During the 1900s, calculators, which are really mini computers, were finally invented.

Calculators vary in their design and in the kinds of problems they can solve.

display

divide

on button

multiply

square root

add

percent

subtract

OFF

off button

total

decimal point

3 The Computer

The First Computers

The first electronic computers were built in the early 1900s. They were used mostly in wartime to break enemy codes.

Computers were enormous, expensive machines. They had to be kept in very large refrigerated rooms. They were sold mostly to governments and businesses and were much too big and expensive for home use.

In the 1960s, transistors were invented and used to build computers. Transistors helped scientists reduce the size of the old giant computers. When transistors were packed on chips, the computer revolution began.

monitor

Modern Computers

Computers today come in three basic kinds: *mainframe, mini,* and *micro.* The computers we have in our homes are microcomputers. Although mainframe, mini, and microcomputers look very different, they are all programmable information-processing machines.

Programmable means that the computer can be told to follow sets of instructions, called *programs*. Once the computer is programmed, it will follow the instructions, or process the information in the program. *System* means a set of separate *components,* or items, that work together to process data.

CPU

Software

The instructions given to the computer are called *software.* Software is written in one of many high-level languages, such as BASIC, Pascal, and C. A compiler or interpreter translates the program language into the *binary code,* or machine language.

cable

Hardware

The processing components of a computer are called the *hardware*. The hardware includes internal memory, the central processing unit, or CPU, storage devices, and input/output devices.

The basic part of both internal memory and the CPU are *semiconductor chips.* These chips are tiny integrated electrical circuits. The circuits on the chips are either "on" or "off." "On" is 1 and "off" is 0 in base 2, or the *binary system* (see Basc 2, p.19). All instructions and data are encoded in the binary system for processing by the CPU. The alphabet, words, and numbers are also encoded in base 2.

Internal memory stores the instructions, or programs, as well as data on chips. Internal memory is either random access memory (RAM) or read-only memory (ROM).

The CPU carries out, or processes, the instructions given in programs. The CPU follows the instructions stored in internal memory to process the data, which is also stored in internal memory. Chips are used in the CPU to process data.

Storage devices include external memory devices such as hard disks, floppy disks, CD-ROM disks, and magnetic tapes. Input devices include keyboards, joysticks, and mice. Output devices include the visual display units, or VDUs, printers, and modems.

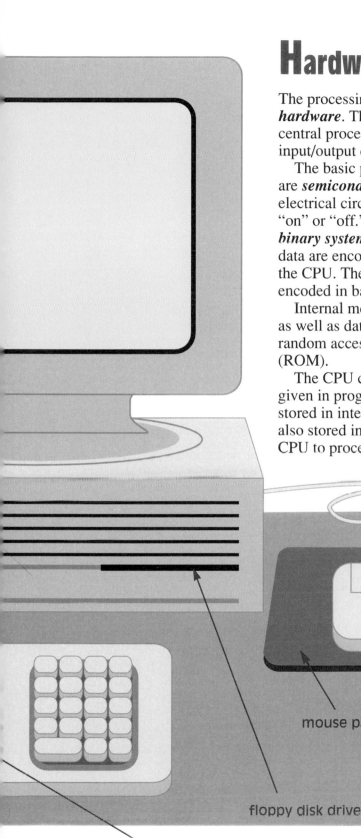

mouse pad

mouse

floppy disk drive

keyboard

INDEX

g

f

h